Population Economics

Research on population economics deals with some of the most pertinent issues of our time and, as such, is of interest to academics and policymakers alike. Like the Journal of Population Economics, the book series "Population Economics" addresses a wide range of theoretical and empirical topics related to all areas of the economics of population, household, and human resources. Books in the series comprise work that closely examines special topics related to population economics, incorporating the most recent developments in the field and the latest research methodologies. Micro-level investigations include topics related to individual, household or family behavior, such as migration, aging, household formation, marriage, divorce, fertility choices, labor supply, health, and risky behavior. Macro-level inquiries examine topics such as economic growth with exogenous or endogenous population evolution, population policy, savings and pensions, social security, housing, and healthcare. These and other topics related to the relationship between population dynamics and public choice, economic approaches to human biology, and the impact of population on income and wealth distributions have important individual, social, and institutional consequences, and their scientific examination informs both economic theory and public policy.

All books in this series are peer-reviewed.

Alessandro Balestrino

The Economics of Family Taxation

Optimal Tax Issues from a Household Economics Perspective

Springer

Alessandro Balestrino
Department of Political Science
University of Pisa
Pisa, Italy

ISSN 1431-6978
Population Economics
ISBN 978-3-031-28169-3 ISBN 978-3-031-28170-9 (eBook)
https://doi.org/10.1007/978-3-031-28170-9

This Springer imprint is published by the registered company Springer Nature Switzerland AG
The registered company address is: Gewerbestrasse 11, 6330 Cham, Switzerland

Preface

In this book, I will try to offer a comprehensive view of the optimal taxation of the family under two main assumptions. First, that fertility is endogenous: parents choose how many children to have. Second, that parents act non-cooperatively: each partner takes the other partner's actions as given when making a choice themselves. The basis for these two main assumptions is factual. Fertility has never reached its theoretical maximum throughout history, and therefore it is immediate to suggest that it must have always been controlled somehow, however imperfectly. Also, enforceable contracts cannot be written within a family: hence, non-cooperative behaviour is a fairly obvious hypothesis to make in order to account for how decisions are taken. We will discuss the assumptions and their bases at length in Chap. 1.

The two assumptions are often used alternatively, that is when the focus is on fertility, the latter is taken to be endogenous, but parents are assumed to act unitarily or cooperatively, whereas when the focus is on parental behaviour, fertility is removed from the picture or taken to be endogenous. This serves the dual purpose of keeping the models manageable and of highlighting the role of each assumption in shaping the structure of taxation. The merging of the two assumptions in a single model is discussed in the last chapter.

The book starts from presenting the standard single-agent framework where taxation issues are usually debated and then illustrates how to expand it by introducing, in a series of steps, home production, non-cooperative partners and endogenous fertility. This is done in Chaps. 2–6. The analytical framework is the same throughout: this way, it is easier to see how each new addition to the model affects the result. We consider different optimal (i.e., Pareto- or welfare-maximising) policies: income taxation, commodity taxation and the taxation of children. For direct and indirect taxation, we highlight the differences relative to the standard case, which are many and rather relevant for policy. For the taxation of children, a constant finding throughout the whole range of variations of the model is that it is difficult to make a case for subsidising fertility when either basic assumption is employed. This is in contrast, clearly, with the standard practice of many real-world governments: the conclusion that must be drawn from our analysis is not, however, that such a practice must be abandoned, rather that it cannot be based on the idea that it is somehow

Pareto- or welfare-improving for the households. Other motivations can however be found.

To the best of my knowledge, an attempt at drawing such a comprehensive picture of the taxation of the family under the two aforementioned assumptions has not been made before. Indeed, optimal taxation is still often studied and taught with a focus on single agents. When "family taxation" is discussed, the members of the couple are commonly taken to act unitarily or cooperatively, and fertility behaviour is rarely, if at all, considered. However, in practice, most real-world agents live in households, and the interaction with the other members affects their behaviour: tax analysis cannot ignore this if the aim is to provide results which are useful for policy prescriptions.

In this book, I draw largely on my own contributions: this is of course not because I am vain, but because I am most familiar with them. The authors whose work has helped me to create mine are fully acknowledged in the book. And, indeed, many of those I have called "my" contributions are co-authored. I take this opportunity to thank Dan Anderberg, Fredrik Andersson, Alessandro Cigno and Anna Pettini, who have worked with me on these issues for years. In most papers, I am no longer able to distinguish my ideas from theirs, and this is as it should be: those articles were born out of our interacting thoughts and there are no separate parts belonging to any of us. In this sense, they also "co-wrote" the present book.

However, my deepest thanks go to Alessandro Petretto, who was my supervisor for my Ph.D. thesis at the University of Sienna and has taught me everything there is to know about optimal tax theory and public economics in general. Subsequently, when I was a young researcher at the University of Pisa, I had the good fortune of meeting Alessandro Cigno, who, in turn, taught me everything there is to know about family economics. From there, the decision to mix the two fields has been a complete no-brainer. Without the two Alessandro's, I would not have been able to write the book.

Indeed, it was Alessandro Cigno who originally suggested that I should write it. As a matter of fact, it was so long ago that he probably does not even remember it. Unfortunately, several things have been hampering my progress on the book: personal losses, as well as the nitty-gritty details of everyday's life (including the pandemics), and of course many, many work engagements. The publisher has been endlessly patient with my delays, and this is something that I appreciate enormously: I really must thank them for that. I would especially like to thank Niko Chtouris for his gentle encouragement and support.

Sadly, the completion of this book has coincided with the news of the passing of one of the most important contributors to the field, Ray Rees. His papers, often co-written with Patricia Apps, have been very influential in family economics, and we all who are currently working in the area owe him a great deal of gratitude for his insightful research. My first encounter with Ray, as a student, was through his excellent microeconomics handbook (co-written with Hugh Gravelle); several years later, in the mid-noughties, I had the pleasure to meet him for the first time in person at a CESifo workshop, when he was teaching at LMU in Munich. As we were both CESifo fellows, we would then see each other often in the subsequent years, and I learned that he was not only an outstanding economist but also an extremely nice and kind person. We all miss him.

Finally, I thank my family with all my heart: they have been a constant support for me in the periods in which I have worked on the book, as they always are for everything. My understanding of family economics has been deepened by the conversations that I have had over the years with my wife, Cinzia Ciardi, who also co-authored a few papers with me on the subject, although in different areas, and brought a new perspective from sociology and, mostly, social psychology. The overall influence of this collaboration and of the constant exchange of ideas over more than two decades is certainly reflected in the approach I have taken to re-elaborate the old material for the present book, especially in the last chapter which has newer content relative to the others. Also, clearly, the overall results and exposition have benefited from such an influence as well as from the resulting interaction with ideas coming from other disciplines. I owe Cinzia very many thanks for this, and, of course, for everything else!

Pisa, Italy
January 2023

Alessandro Balestrino

Contents

Chapter 1
Standard Optimal Taxation with Single Agents: What It Is and What to Use in Its Place

This chapter purports to accomplish two objectives: first, to give a brief summary of how optimal tax theory works when applied to a world with individual agents whose time allocation choices are limited to labour and leisure, and, second, to illustrate why it is better not to use this variant, but rather focus on a more general approach where (i) economic agents are households, and (ii) there are multiple uses of time—an approach of which the standard setup would indeed be a special case. From a pedagogical viewpoint, the analysis of such a standard setup would however retain its value as a benchmark against which to appreciate the strength of the wider approach with multi-agent economic subjects and fully modelled time allocation; it is in this spirit that we will proceed in what follow.

1.1 A Brief Synthesis of Standard Optimal Tax Theory

In the standard optimal tax analysis households are made of just one person and their time can be allocated to either one of two uses, labour or leisure. This topic is in fact well-known and has been presented not only in original works (Ramsey, 1927; Mirrlees, 1971, 1976; Atkinson, 1977; Atkinson & Stiglitz, 1976; Stern, 1982, Stiglitz, 1982, Christiansen, 1984) but also in established handbooks (e.g. Myles, 2012; Atkinson & Stiglitz, 1981, 2015). For this reason we will limit ourselves to a relatively quick exposition that emphasises the intuition behind the results rather than the technicalities: those who desire a more rounded-up presentation are referred to the works cited above and the references therein.

This chapter will be based mostly on Edwards et al. (1994) and Nava et al. (1996), especially the former, which provide a very clear and intuitive synthesis of how the whole optimal tax structure can be derived. Edwards et al. (1994) focus on a so-called mixed tax system, i.e. a combination of non-linear income tax and linear commodity taxes that is possibly the best way to model actual tax structures, in which

A. Balestrino, *The Economics of Family Taxation*, Population Economics,
https://doi.org/10.1007/978-3-031-28170-9_1

progressive direct taxes are normally accompanied by proportional indirect taxes. The exact nature of the mixed tax system depends on the information that is assumed to be available to the government. For example, it is commonly supposed, with reason, that the government cannot identify the purchaser in commodity transactions; this means that such transactions can only be observed anonymously and therefore indirect taxes have to be linear. Another standard assumption is that gross income can be observed[1] (while hours worked or wage rates cannot), so that the government can tax it non-linearly, although it cannot use personalised lump-sum taxes. We will maintain the mixed tax system as the standard tax framework, but we will sometimes revert to a fully linear tax system, in which all tax rates are uniform, when necessary to make a specific point. Since throughout the book we will try to characterise in a variety of settings how an optimal redistributive tax structure must look like, the standard case treated in this chapter provides, as mentioned, a useful benchmark.

1.1.1 The Model

There are two types of individuals, type 1 and type 2; there are n^h agents of each type, $h = 1, 2$. They all have the same utility function defined over M consumption goods x_i and labour l^h:

$$U^h = U(\boldsymbol{x}^h, l^h) \tag{1.1}$$

However, type-2 agents have somehow a higher "ability" and therefore earn a higher pre-tax wage rate $w^2 > w^1$. The tax authority only observes earnings (as we just mentioned, compliance is assumed to be complete), that is $y^h = w^h l^h$, not ability—and does not observe l^h either. Personalised lump-sum taxes based on ability are therefore ruled out: the tax schedule must be designed in such a way that the more convenient choice for the agent is to self-reveal her ability, i.e. it is must be "incentive-compatible".

Let us solve the agent's optimisation problem in two steps. Going backwards, we first see how she can allocate a fixed amount of disposable income b^h over the consumption goods. Letting q_i denote the consumer price of a generic good, the first step amounts to choosing the vector of consumption goods $\boldsymbol{x}^h$ so as to maximise

$$U(\boldsymbol{x}^h, y^h/w^h) \text{ s.t. } \sum_{i=1}^{M} q_i x_i^h = b^h. \tag{1.2}$$

[1] In other words, there is full income tax compliance. Actually, assuming that taxes can be avoided or evaded would not prevent the government from using a non-linear income tax; the effects of reduced tax compliance would however have to be modelled and this would complicate the picture. Also, notice that we implicitly assumed that also for indirect taxes we have full compliance—which is not necessarily the case in actuality.

From this, one can derive the indirect utility function as

$$V^h = V(\boldsymbol{q}, b^h, y^h; w^h). \tag{1.3}$$

It is now important to make an assumption that ensures that type-2 agents always have a higher pre-tax and post-tax income than type-1 agents, otherwise it would be difficult to characterise properly any redistributive policy. A possibility, adopted here, is to assume that the indifference curves in the (y, b)-space are always flatter for high-wage individuals—see Edwards et al. (1994) for details.[2] Formally: $\frac{\partial(-V_y/V_b)}{\partial w} < 0$. On this basis, one can identify the high-ability agents also as the "high-earners".

The demand function stemming from the above maximisation problem,

$$x_i^h\left(\boldsymbol{q}, b^h, y^h; w\right) = -\frac{V_{q^i}}{V_b}, \tag{1.4}$$

can be shown to satisfy the following properties:

$$\sum_{i=1}^{M} q_i \frac{\partial x_i^h}{\partial b^h} = 1; \; \sum_{i=1}^{M} q_i \frac{\partial x_i^h}{\partial y^h} = 0 \tag{1.5}$$

Then, the agents chooses her labour supply, or equivalently, her earnings—it is convenient to use the latter variable as this is what the government observes. So she maximises (1.3) subject to the budget constraint

$$b = y - T(y), \tag{1.6}$$

where $T(y)$ is the non-linear income tax schedule. The FOC is

$$-\frac{V_y}{V_b} = 1 - T'(y), \tag{1.7}$$

where $T'(y)$ is the marginal tax rate.

The income tax is one of the policy instrument in the government's toolbox. It is convenient to characterise it as if the objects of choice for the policy maker were directly b^h and y^h, with the agents selecting the preferred (b, y) pair; one can then identify the marginal tax rates using (1.7). The government has at its disposal also indirect linear taxes t_i; consumer prices are in fact given by

$$q_i = p_i + t_i, \tag{1.8}$$

[2] For $M = 1$, this is known as the agent monotonicity or single-crossing condition (Seade 1982).

where p_i are producer prices, assumed to be constant (that is, all commodities are produced with effective labour as only input and with linear technologies).[3] Sometimes, it may be convenient to set all the producer prices equal to unity, which can be done simply by choosing units appropriately. Only linear taxes can be deployed, as the government can only observe anonymous transactions, i.e. it cannot identify the type of the consumer who makes a purchase.

Let us now define the objective of the government as the identification of a set of second-best Pareto efficient tax rules: that is, the government aims to maximise the utility of type-1 agents V^1 subject to the utility of type-2 agents to be at least a given amount $\overline{V}$. The government faces two constraints.

The first is a revenue constraint:

$$n_1\left(T\left(y^1\right)+\sum_{i=1}^{M} t_i x_i^1(\cdot)\right)+n_2\left(T\left(y^2\right)+\sum_{i=1}^{M} t_i x_i^2(\cdot)\right)=R, \tag{1.9}$$

where R is a fixed revenue requirement and the arguments of the demand functions (1.4) have been ignored to avoid clutter.

The second is in fact a set of constraints, namely the self-selection constraints meant to ensure that the tax rules are such that each type prefers the (b, y) package intended for her over the one intended for the other. Typically, the only case studied is the one in which the redistribution goes from the high- to the low-ability agents, that is the case in which the government has a quasi-concave objective function (or, to use a less technical expression, social preferences exhibit an aversion to inequality: social indifference curves are convex—see e.g. Boadway & Bruce, 1975).

Sometimes, we will make the role of the social welfare function (SWF) more apparent, by explicitly setting it up and deriving the rules for a social optimum, rather than a Pareto optimum *per se*. However, since we employ typical "Paretian" SWFs, which are increasing in all their arguments (namely, individual utilities), any socially optimal outcome is also a Pareto-efficient one. In some cases, this will help us to discuss the equity-efficiency trade-off, as the SWF tries to balance the two objectives. To this end, we will often refer to the two extreme cases of utilitarian (or "Benthamite") and Rawlsian SWF, and compare the outcomes: indeed, the first has straight lines for indifference curves and is therefore concerned exclusively with efficiency, whereas the latter has L-shaped indifference curves and therefore focuses on equity.

---

[3] It turns out that optimal tax analysis is especially simple if one assumes constant returns to scale in the production sector. For one thing this ensures that any tax levied on the production side will be translated 100% forward, which makes it unnecessary to distinguish between production and consumption taxes. More importantly, it freezes any impact that changes in the production (that is, pre-tax) prices may have on the consumer demand. In fact, the latter is in principle homogeneous of degree zero in the vector $(\boldsymbol{q}, I)$, where I is the lump-sum profit distributed by the firms to the consumers. However, with constant returns to scale, $I = 0$ always. Therefore, changes in pre-tax price do not affect either I or the consumer demand functions.

In any case, then, the only binding self-selection constraint will be the one preventing the high-ability agent to "mimick" the low-ability one:

$$V(\boldsymbol{q}, b^2, y^2; w^2) \geq \widehat{V}(\boldsymbol{q}, b^1, y^1; w^2). \tag{1.10}$$

This implies that the optimally chosen taxes must be such that type-2 individuals are better off revealing their true colors rather that posing as type-1 agents, which they could do by earning the same income as the latter (the "hat" denotes the "mimickers").

The Lagrangian of the optimal taxation problem is then

$$\begin{aligned} L = {} & V(\mathbf{q}, b^2, y^2; w^2) + \gamma \left(V(\mathbf{q}, b^1, y^1; w^1) - \bar{V} \right) \\ & + \sigma \left(V(\mathbf{q}, b^2, y^2; w^2) - \hat{V}(\mathbf{q}, b^1, y^1; w^2) \right) \\ & + \mu \left(n^1 \left(y^1 - \sum_{i=1}^{n} p_i x_i^1 \left(\mathbf{q}, b^1, y^1; w^1 \right) \right) \right. \\ & \left. + n^2 \left(y^2 - \sum_{i=1}^{n} p_i x_i^2 \left(\mathbf{q}, b^2, y^2; w^2 \right) \right) - R \right), \end{aligned} \tag{1.11}$$

where the revenue constraint has been rewritten using the agents' budget constraints and γ, σ and μ are Lagrange multipliers. The choice variable are y^h, b^h, and t_i or equivalently q_i, $i = 1, 2 \ldots M$; recall that choosing y and b is the same as choosing $T(y)$. The FOCs are:

$$V_y^1 = \sigma \widehat{V}_y^2 - \mu n^1 \left(1 - \sum_{i=1}^{M} p_i \frac{\partial x_i^1}{\partial y^1} \right); \tag{1.12}$$

$$V_b^1 = \sigma \widehat{V}_y^2 + \mu n^1 \sum_{i=1}^{M} p_i \frac{\partial x_i^1}{\partial b^1}; \tag{1.13}$$

$$(\gamma + \sigma) V_y^2 = -\mu n^2 \left(1 - \sum_{i=1}^{M} p_i \frac{\partial x_i^2}{\partial y^2} \right); \tag{1.14}$$

$$(\gamma + \sigma) V_b^2 = \mu n^2 \sum_{i=1}^{M} p_i \frac{\partial x_i^2}{\partial b^2}; \tag{1.15}$$

$$-V_b^1 x_i^1 - (\gamma + \sigma) V_b^2 x_i^2 + \sigma \widehat{V}_b^2 \widehat{x}_i^2 - \mu \sum_{h=1}^{2} n^i \sum_{j=1}^{M} p_j \frac{\partial x_j^h}{\partial q_i} = 0, \; i = 1, 2 \ldots \text{M}. \tag{1.16}$$

Notice that the last expression has been derived by using (1.4).

1.1.2 The Tax Rules

I will now state the main results concerning the tax rates, without however providing any proof. These are, as I said, established results and the interest reader can find the relevant demonstrations in the literature cited above. Also, as standard in optimal tax theory, I simply assume that a solution exists, as the optimisation problem is not necessarily well-behaved.

First, define the total tax paid at income y as

$$\Theta\left(y^h\right) = T\left(y^h\right) + \sum_{i=1}^{M} t_i x_i^h\left(\boldsymbol{q}, y^h, y^h - T\left(y^h\right); w^h\right) \tag{1.17}$$

and, consequently, the marginal effective tax rate as

$$\Theta'\left(y^h\right) = T' + \sum_{i=1}^{M} t_i \left(\frac{\partial x_i^h}{\partial b^h}\left(1 - T'\right) + \frac{\partial x_i^h}{\partial y^h}\right). \tag{1.18}$$

At the optimum, one can show by appropriately manipulating the first four FOCs that

$$\Theta'\left(y^2\right) = 0,\ \Theta'\left(y^1\right) = \frac{\sigma \widehat{V}_b^2}{\mu n^1}\left(\frac{\widehat{V}_y^2}{\widehat{V}_b^2} - \frac{V_y^1}{V_b^1}\right) > 0, \tag{1.19}$$

where the sign for the second result follows by the single-crossing condition (see fn. 2). Because type-1 individuals have the same y, b and clearly face the same $\mathbf{q}$ as mimicking type-2 individuals, but enjoy a lower wage (also, σ and μ are both positive).

In words, the high-ability agents face a zero marginal *effective* tax rate, while the low-ability ones face a positive tax rate. The first part implies that the marginal *income* tax rate is not in general zero for the high-earners; however, the distortions imposed by the two parts of the tax system, i.e. direct and indirect taxes, average out, so that if the high-ability agents earn a little more they end up paying the same total amount of taxes. Indeed, were not that the case, it would be possible to devise a small tax reform such that the total revenue increases leaving the high-earners welfare unchanged and consequently not inducing any mimicking behaviour. We would not then be at a Pareto optimum. On the other hand, the low-earners' tax debts will rise whenever their incomes rise, as expected: the positive marginal tax rate is intended to discourage mimicking.

As for the indirect taxes, the relevant rule, obtained by an appropriate manipulation of the last FOC, is as follows:

$$n^1 \sum_{j=1}^{M} t_j \frac{\partial \widetilde{x}_j^1}{\partial q_i} + n^2 \sum_{j=1}^{M} t_j \frac{\partial \widetilde{x}_j^2}{\partial q_i} = \sigma \frac{\widehat{V}_b^2}{\mu}\left(x_h^1 - \widehat{x}_h^2\right),\ i = 1, 2 \ldots \mathrm{M}, \tag{1.20}$$

where the "tilde" denotes the compensated conditional demand. That is, the change in the aggregated compensated demand brought about by a marginal variation in the commodity tax rates (sometimes called the "discouragement index") must be proportional to the difference between the demand by the actual type-1 agent and the the demand by the mimicker. In other words, the indirect tax must discourage mimicking behaviour by taxing more heavily those goods that are used by the mimicker more than her genuine type-1 counterpart. Notice that the mimicker works less than the type-1 agent, because she has a higher wage and the same income; therefore, the more heavily taxed goods will be those that exhibit a stronger complementarity with leisure—where complementarity is defined at the level of the conditional demand functions (1.4) used here.

Summing up, the nature of the optimal redistributive tax structure can be defined by underlining a couple of features that are implicit in its second-best setting, as they mostly concern the role of distortions. First, we have an extended version of the "no-distortion at the top" result, usually referred to income taxes alone[4] (e.g. Stiglitz 1982): here it is shown to involve the whole tax system and is achieved, as mentioned, through the action of countervailing distortions. Second, indirect taxes are shown to have a dual role, in that they impose a distortion on the agents' choices in order to (i) discourage mimicking, and (ii) mitigate the negative impact of the income tax on the labour supply by hitting more heavily goods which are, in a precise sense, complementary to leisure.

1.1.3 A Simpler Setting: Linear Income Taxation

Sometimes, it might be appropriate (e.g. to simplify the setup) to use a less general tax framework, that is one in which also the income tax is linear, i.e. identified by a constant marginal tax rate τ and a uniform lump-sum subsidy T; in that case, the self-selection constraint will be non-binding. The agent's problem would then be

$$\max U(\mathbf{x}^h, l^h) \text{ s.t. } \sum_{i=1}^{n} q_i x_i^h = (1-\tau)w^h l^h + T. \tag{1.21}$$

This can be solved in one go, and yields the following indirect utility function:

$$V^h = V\left(\mathbf{q}, \tau, T; w^h\right). \tag{1.22}$$

[4] As is well-known, not too much must be read into this result; certainly it cannot be interpreted as supporting the idea that actual income tax rates must be low at the top of the income redistribution. Indeed, real-world income tax schedules are normally built around a multi-bracket system, so that the top marginal rate applies to a group of agents with different income, a feature that alone invalidates the "no-distortion at the top" results (see e.g. Atkinson & Stiglitz, 1981, 2015). Within the logic of the model, the high-earners face a zero marginal tax rate simply because no-one tries to mimick them.

This setup can be further simplified using our assumption of constant return to scale, which allows us to do two things at once: first, normalise the vector of production prices and choose a *numeraire*; second, normalise the vector of production prices and choose an untaxed good. Since the two normalisation processes do not interfere with each other, any good can be the *numeraire* and the untaxed good at the same time. this highlights the fact that, in a general equilibrium perspective, only relative prices matter; the optimal tax design gives prescriptions in terms of relative, as opposed to absolutee, prices.

The reason why this matters in this context (while it was not brought up when discussing the mixed tax system above) is that a common choice for the untaxed good—when the tax system is linear—is leisure, in which case we cannot derive an explicit rule for the income tax: we can only say whether a given commodity is taxed more leniently or more heavily than leisure. The choice of leisure is by no means necessary, however: in fact, when the model is further simplified to include only one consumption good, this good is usually chosen as both the *numeraire* and the untaxed good, so that the income tax rule can be clearly identified. Let us then take up these two cases in turn.

When $\tau = 0$, the indirect utility function is simply

$$V^h = V\left(\mathbf{q}, T; w^h\right); \tag{1.23}$$

as mentioned, the government faces just one constraint in defining the second-best Pareto efficient tax rules, namely the budget constraint:

$$n^1 . \sum_{i=1}^{M} t_i x_i^1(\cdot) + n^2 \sum_{i=1}^{M} t_i x_i^2(\cdot) = T. \tag{1.24}$$

On the other hand, when $M = 1$ and $t_1 = 0$, the indirect utility function and the government budget constraint are, respectively:

$$V^h = V\left(\tau, T; w^h\right), \tag{1.25}$$

$$\tau\left(n^1 w^1 l^1 + n^2 w^2 l^2\right) = T. \tag{1.26}$$

It is then possible to derive the optimal tax rules for the two cases. As before, we just give the results without the details, which can be found in advanced textbooks such as Myles (2008). Indeed, we state immediately the tax *formulae*.

Let us start from the first case:

$$D_k \equiv \frac{n^1 \sum_{i=1}^{M} t_i \frac{\partial \tilde{x}_j^1}{\partial q_i} + n^2 \sum_{i=1}^{M} \frac{\partial \tilde{x}_j^2}{\partial q_i}}{n^1 x_j^1 + n^1 x_j^2} = -\left(1 - r_j\right), \tag{1.27}$$

where the upper bar denotes an average value and

$$\beta^1 = \frac{V_T^1}{\mu} + n^1 \sum_{i=1}^{M} t_i \frac{\partial x_i^1}{\partial T} + n^2 \sum_{i=1i}^{M} \frac{\partial x_i^2}{\partial T}; \tag{1.28}$$

$$\beta^2 = \gamma \frac{V_T^2}{\mu} + n^1 \sum_{i=1i}^{M} \frac{\partial x_i^1}{\partial T} + n^2 \sum_{i=1i}^{M} \frac{\partial x_i^2}{\partial T} \tag{1.29}$$

are the social net marginal utilities of income: "social" because they include the marginal social value of the public funds (i.e. μ, the Lagrange multiplier of the revenue constraint) and "net" because they also include the effects on revenue of a marginal increase in the agent's income. The term on the l.h.s is (a variant of) the so-called index of discouragement as defined above, i.e. a measure of the reduction of compensated demand due to taxation. As for the term on the r.h.s., we can write

$$r_j = 1 + cov\left(\beta, x_j\right) \tag{1.30}$$

where cov denotes covariance, and r is the so-called redistributive characteristic of good j, whose value exceeds (falls short of) unity if j is consumed prevalently by the households with low (high) β. It is normally assumed that β is non-increasing in w, that is that one extra-euro assigned to the low-earner is seen as socially more valuable than one extra-euro assigned to the high-earner. In turn, the assumption that β is non-increasing in w is basically an assumption that income effects of taxation are negligible, for then the second and third term in the expression for β are dominated by the first: then, if the private marginal utility of income (V_T) is non-increasing in w, so is β. So, the rules require that indirect taxes are designed in such a way that the consumption of commodity k is encouraged (discouraged) if it is mostly demanded by the relatively poor, high-β (relatively well-off, low-β) families.

As for the second case, i.e. when $M = 1$ and $t_1 = 0$, let us denote the compensated labour supply elasticities w.r.t. the net wage rate with e_l^h and define

$$E_l = -\sum_{h=1}^{2} n^h y^h e_l^h < 0. \tag{1.31}$$

as (minus) the weighted average of such elasticities. Then, we have

$$\frac{\tau}{1-\tau} = \frac{cov(\beta, y)}{-E_l}. \tag{1.32}$$

Note that this is just an implicit solution; we can however establish whether τ is included between 0 and 1. Actually, since $E_l < 0$, it follows that, for t to be between 0 and 1, it is sufficient that $cov(\beta, y) \leq 0$. This latter condition is satisfied if β is non-increasing in w, that we just saw is commonly taken to be the case.

1.2 What to Use in Place of the Standard Framework

As mentioned, the above analysis is lacking on at least two counts: first, it is based on the assumption that individuals constitute the significant economic unit, which is not really consistent with the common-sense observation that most people live in households; second, it restricts arbitrarily the time allocation process to a binary choice, either labour or leisure, ignoring other obvious uses of time such as home-production.

Of course these two aspects are linked: if one believes that the appropriate setup for framing policy questions in general (as well as the specific optimal taxation issues in which we are interested here) is provided by household production models *à la* Becker (1981), it comes natural to assume that the relevant economic subjects, i.e. households, are composed of multiple agents and/or that there can be multiple uses of time. Notice that I wrote "and/or" because it is sometimes (although not always—see below) possible to introduce one of the two extensions without the other. For example, one can have a single-agent model in which there are three or more uses of time, as in the path-breaking contributions by Becker (1965) and Gronau (1977). Indeed, we will devote the next chapter to the study of optimal taxation within such a framework. However, when multi-agent households are considered, things become a little more complicated.

To see this, notice that the household economics models are usually geared to deal with either intergenerational or intragenerational issues, rarely both. It is convenient, for the purpose of a clearer exposition, to discuss the two variants separately. Indeed, the models differ in their structure in that those meant to study intragenerational issues depart from the single-agent approach by considering, typically, *two decision-makers* within the family, often with no children; whereas those intended for approaching intergenerational issues, usually assume that there are *two generations* in the family, i.e. parents and children—but normally the parents act unitarily and the children are all identical. Now, when discussing the intragenerational models, it will be possible to set aside the issue of time allocation—these models can retain the standard labour-leisure dichotomy. Instead, in the case of the intergenerational models, allowing for different uses of time becomes an indispensable part of the modelling strategy, an obvious reason being the need for the adults to devote some time to child-rearing—which, as everybody who has children knows, is often far from a leisurely activity.

1.2.1 Intragenerational Issues

The first attempts at modelling family decision-making, originating from Becker's (1965) and Gronau's (1977) models of time allocation, have been part of the so-called unitary approach, in which households are seen as having a single objective function despite being made of more than one member. This latter view is for example adopted by Becker (1981) under an umbrella assumption that economic agents are selfish in the marketplace but altruistic within the family: there is a benevolent head—a *pater familias* if you will—who coordinates every member's preferences by means of household welfare function, that in turn can then be interpreted as the utility function of a unitary entity. In this case, the above standard optimal tax analysis would apply basically unchanged—although it still would yield original results due to the richer structure of time allocation (see below and the next chapter).

The defining characteristic of the unitary approach is that it views the family as an efficient decision-maker. There are at least two other approaches that share this feature with the unitary approach: they are the "cooperative bargaining approach" and the "collective approach", respectively.[5]

The former goes back to the the static Nash bargaining models of Manser and Brown (1980) and McElroy and Horney (1981). These were criticised because static bargaining requires that the parties, here the partners in the married or however cohabiting couple, are able to reach binding agreements; however, it is highly implausible that legally enforceable contracts can be written within the family—see e.g. Cigno (1991, 1993, 2006) and Anderberg and Balestrino (2003). A possible defense would be to argue that the static Nash bargaining model can be viewed as the limiting case of a dynamic alternating offers model with risk of breakdown and discounting in which the time intervals between offers have become vanishingly small (Binmore et al., 1986). This line of defence would however work only in a stationary environment, which hardly seems the case in a marriage. Indeed, one can think of many events which have the potential to alter the environment irreversibly. Imagine for example a situation in which a couple has been given the possibility to move to another city: this would allow one of the partners to take up a very promising job offer, but at same time it would force the other partner to leave her or his own job. Clearly, no matter whether the couple decides to move or not, the outcome of the process would radically alter the distribution of bargaining power between the partners.

The "collective approach" has been developed instead by Chiappori (1988, 1992), Browning and Chiappori (1998), Chiappori et al. (2002), Bourguignon et al. (2006) and Browning and Gørtz (2012), and widely explored also in connection with tax issues, see e.g. Apps and Rees (1999, 2011, 2018).[6] In this case, efficiency is postulated at the outset on the basis of the assumption that a marriage is a prototypical example of game-theoretic repeated interaction, and therefore ought to sustain efficient outcomes by the folk theorem. This argument is however not entirely convincing, for two reasons. First, the folk theorem does not ensure that the efficient outcomes are the only equilibria, nor that they will be more likely to occur than the inefficient ones. Second, it is far from clear that an approach based on repeated interaction is a plausible modelling choice, as there are many important areas of family life for which decision reversal is costly (e.g. the decision to move to another town or to accept a specific job offer or to attend a professional training course, etc.) or impossible (e.g. the decision to inoculate themselves against infective illnesses). Indeed, Lundberg

[5] For a survey of models of efficient decision-making within the household, see Vermeulen (2002).

[6] An in-depth review of family taxation issues within the unitary, collective and bargaining models of the family is Rees (2023).

and Pollak (2003), working *within the bargaining approach*, propose to think of marriages not as repeated games, but as non-stationary, multi-stage games, because many decisions in a marriage may affect the future bargaining power structure; in the absence of a commitment mechanism, then, inefficient outcomes are permissible.[7]

It seems then fair to say that there are several theoretical arguments undermining the belief that families choices are always efficient. On top of them, one could also add arguments based on empirical evidence. For example, the study of divorce behaviour under changes in divorce legislation has shown a tendency for the divorce rate to increase in the presence of a move to unilateral divorce law—see Friedberg (1998) and Gruber (2000). But, if families are efficient decision-makers also divorces should be the outcome of an efficient decision; then, we should not observe any change in divorce behaviour when no-fault divorce is introduced. Another point is that efficiency requires that household members fully pool their incomes, which is not well-confirmed empirically—see e.g. Lundberg and Pollak (2007), Ponthieux (2013) and Barcena-Martin et al. (2020).

For all these reasons, then, a simple non-cooperative approach relying on the standard Nash equilibrium concept in the spirit of Wolley (1988), Konrad and Lommerud (1995) and Anderberg and Balestrino (2007, 2011), looks rather promising as an immediate way to model the process whereby couples can arrive at a common decision—actually, the approach can be traced back to Becker (1974). None of the critiques above apply, and, also, the non-cooperative approach captures immediately the fact that reasonable outcomes should be self-enforcing, since, as mentioned, it is impossible to write binding contracts regulating intrafamily behaviour. As a consequence, we have to abandon the idea that families are efficient decision-makers. We will develop an optimal taxation analysis for this case in Chap. 3.

1.2.2 Intergenerational Issues

As mentioned, whenever intergenerational issues are studied, the standard approach is to posit that there are two generations living together in a family, parents and children: parents act unitarily and are in fact often modelled as a female agent, as such referred to as "she", while children are all identical. This is of course done for reasons of simplicity and manageability; however, it should be noted that this approach prejudges the question whether parents act cooperatively or not by assuming that the former is always the case. Inasmuch as the present book reviews and summarises existing literature, I will of course conform to this usage. In the final chapter I will try however to see what the implications are of assuming non-cooperative behaviour in reproductive matters.

[7] Lundberg and Pollak, in a previous contribution (Lundberg and Pollak, 1993), also adopted the bargaining approach, but modelled the threat point as a non-cooperative equilibrium, so that the equilibrium of the bargaining game, in case of very large transaction costs, was in fact the inefficient threat point.

Within the standard framework there is of course room for several variants: we may have overlapping generations models or finite-horizon models; we may have altruistic parents or selfish parents; sometimes also children are altruistic towards the parents, sometimes not; parents may be able to choose how many children they have (so-called "endogenous fertility models") or they may not be able ("exogenous fertility models"), and so on and so forth. However, the main distinctions are in fact two.

The first distinction is between the models in which parents are seen as altruistic and those in which they are seen as selfish (this mirrors the non-cooperative vs. cooperative dichotomy). In the first case children are seen as "consumption goods", i.e. the parents "enjoy" them as such; in the second case, instead, they are seen as "investment goods", i.e. the parents expect a "return" from them, such as assistance in their old age. The policy implications, for one, may vary significantly but a consensus on which is the most plausible setup has not been reached. In particular, the results from the empirical literature are hardly decisive. It is true that the testable implications of the altruistic model are usually not verified: e.g. Altonji et al. (1992, 1997) find that the usual test of altruistic behaviour (namely that an increase of one monetary unit in the income of the child, accompanied by a decrease of one monetary unit in the income of the parent, should lead to one monetary unit reduction in the transfers) fails to hold. Instead, the testable implications of the exchange model are not usually contradicted by the empirical findings: e.g. Cigno et al. (1998, 2006) perform a test based on the effect of a binding credit ration on the probability of making a money transfer and find that the result is compatible with the assumption that individuals optimise subject to a self-enforcing family constitution specifying the rules for the intergenerational transfers. It has however been argued that the test usually employed for the altruistic model is unnecessarily restrictive: specifically, McGarry (2000) notices that the test is conceived in such a way that it cannot but fail as long as parents use observations on the current incomes of children to update their expectations about future incomes. So, its failure does not *per se* implies that altruism is not present. We can conclude that at this stage of our general knowledge there is no definitive case in favour of one or the other approach.

The second distinction is between the exogenous and the endogenous fertility approaches. Here, it is easier to reach a conclusion, as there is an argument in favor of endogenous fertility that is, in my view, just as simple as is powerful: the total fertility rates actually observed never reach the maximum possible rate, hence households control the number of children they have (Dasgupta 2000). Such control, of course, does not have to be perfect for the argument to maintain its force. Not all the couples may be able to control their fertility completely. For example, some couples might have less children than planned—which is basically equivalent to experience exogenous fertility. Or, couples may make mistakes in the opposite direction, to wit they might have more children than planned. Moreover, it is always possible, I believe, to justify the assumption of exogenous fertility whenever it helps to keep the model manageable in cases in which the main focus of the research is on other issues.

In the following chapters, therefore, I will review models with altruistic parents and others with selfish parents, as well as models with endogenous fertility and others with exogenous fertility, depending on the circumstances. In all cases, however, children will be considered as valuable, be that as a consumption or as an investment good, by their parents. This rules out any consideration of the "equivalence scales" literature, which, as is well-known, focuses on how the tax treatment of families must be adjusted to account for different sizes, in particular oh how large families must be compensated for the greater costs they face—see for example Deaton and Muellbauer (1980). In that literature, indeed, it is always assumed that children have no value whatsoever for their parents and, also, that fertility is exogenous. Moreover, this is often done implicitly, as if it were not even worth discussing. In fact, the need for large families to be compensated is taken for granted and the model is built accordingly, assuming from the start that children are simply a cost that the parents incur without having any control on it. The real aim is to pinpoint the exact level of the compensation for different numbers of children. Unfortunately, this means that children are treated like disabling accidents. I would argue, instead, that this is one of the cases in which the assumption of exogenous fertility is not tenable, because clearly fertility here is the main issue under consideration and its nature must be modelled accurately; secondly, and relatedly, once fertility is correctly defined as endogenous, it is difficult to imagine how a couple could decide to have a child if it had no value to them. Balestrino, (2015) provides an analysis of how families of different size should be treated within a redistributive tax system and finds that, in a (plausible) setup in which parents value their children and fertility is generally endogenous but some couples are constrained by reproductive limits or inadvertently end up with more children than planned, compensations are not due to large families as such but those which are too small or too large as defined above: moreover, in practice, such compensations might not be awarded because it is not always possible to ascertain if a family is indeed of the "wrong" size or just claims to be. This contradicts, then, the common policy implications of the equivalence scales literature.

Chapter 2
Optimal Taxation in the Presence of Household Production

At the end of Chap. 1, we stressed that the main role of commodity taxation in a Pareto-optimal second-best tax system is an efficiency one: it counteracts the distortions away from market work and towards leisure inevitably brought about by the income tax as it performs its redistributive role. Within the limits of the standard model, there is a significant exception, known as the Atkinson-Stiglitz theorem (Atkinson and Stiglitz 1976) which states that if the government can implement a non-linear income tax and if commodities are weakly separable from leisure in the utility function, then commodity taxes are not needed for attaining a second-best Pareto optimum.

The reason is clear: weak separability prevents indirect taxes from performing their counter-distortionary role. This result has been highly influential and has helped to cast some doubts on the effectiveness and indeed the relevance of commodity taxes in the real world. Interestingly, however, once household production is introduced, that is once non-working time is supposed to be used, in combination with purchased inputs, to produce domestically one or more final consumption goods, the whole analysis must be reframed. The first author to deal with this subject has been, to the best of our knowledge, Sandmo (1990),[1] who, employing a model in which tradeable commodities can be either purchased on the market or produced domestically, discusses the efficient tax treatment of two types of goods: (i) market substitutes for household-produced commodities and (ii) inputs into the home-production process. The standard conclusion that commodity taxes counteract the distortion towards leisure implied by the income tax cannot be replicated here, inasmuch as there is no leisure in a strictly Beckerian model; but even if one were to use the Grounau (1977) specification, that allows for leisure to be present along with domestic production, the conclusion needs to be qualified. Also, the Atkinson-Stiglitz cannot survive as it is in this setting. When household production is taken into account, a subset of the commodities will be naturally related to the household production process, either as

[1] See also Rosen (1995) and Kleven et al. (1999). For a general survey of economic models of the family, see Apps and Rees (2023).

A. Balestrino, *The Economics of Family Taxation*, Population Economics,
https://doi.org/10.1007/978-3-031-28170-9_2

input goods or as market substitutes. Therefore, there are theoretical reasons why separability of all goods from all uses on non-market hours is implausible; but, as we shall see, even if were to allow it, there will in general be a role for commodity taxes.

Indeed, Sandmo (1990) argues that since the household production activity cannot be monitored by the tax authorities, there is a case for adjusting the taxation of those commodities that are somehow related to it (such as, indeed, market substitutes and inputs), no matter whether they have any relation to leisure. In particular, he makes a case based on efficiency reasons: taxing home-production inputs heavily as well as market substitutes lightly would counteract the distortions away from market work and towards home-work generated by the income tax. Interestingly, the recommendation differs from the standard one, but it follows the same logic: commodity taxes must counteract the distorsions created by the income tax. It is indeed yet another application of a general principle, sometimes known as the Theorem of the Second Best, which tells us that in an economy in which distortions are present and cannot be removed, it is in general optimal to have countervailing distortions in place.

In this chapter we will amalgamate Sandmo's model with the ones used by Anderberg and Balestrino (2000) and Balestrino et al. (2003) (which are in turn based, to differing extents, on Sandmo 1990 as well as on Cigno 2001), in order to present a general analysis of optimal taxation in the presence of household production. The analysis has three main characteristics:

(i) it focuses on redistribution as well as efficiency: to this end, we will use a tax model inspired by the standard one presented in Chap. 1, in which the available set of policies is restricted only by the information available to the government (personalised lump-sum taxes and non-linear indirect taxes are thus ruled out);
(ii) it includes the case in which the home-produced good is tradeable, and, therefore, has a perfect substitute available on the market, but it is mostly based on the one in which it is *not* tradeable (this latter case covers, among other things, the situation in which households are made of couples acting unitarily and the domestically produced goods are children);
(iii) households are conceived as at least potentially differing along two dimensions, that is market ability (as we had in Chap. 1) as well as home production ability, with differing types of correlation between the two abilities.

2.1 Indirect Taxation in the Presence of Home-Production

To begin with, we will focus on a case in which the government has a redistributive objective, domestically produced goods are not tradeable (thus, there are no perfect substitutes on the market), and agents differ only in terms of their market ability. This way, the model is the same as in Chap. 1, but household production is now included. So, there are two types of individuals in the economy, low- and high-ability households, $h = 1, 2$ with n^h households of each type, $n^1 + n^2 = 1$; type-2 households earn a higher pre-tax wage rate $w^2 > w^1$. The time endowment is normalized to unity and it is allocated to market labour l and two non-market uses, leisure L and home-time λ; pre-tax income is thus $y = wl$.

Following Gronau (1977), we let leisure enter the utility function and also assume that home-time, λ, is combined with an input good, z, in order to domestically produce a final consumption good, c; the consumption good x, that, like leisure, affects utility directly, is purchased on the market.[2] Of course, this neat partition of marketed commodities between a consumption good and an input good is assumed for the purposes of keeping the model as manageable as possible: in practice, distinguishing them might be more difficult than we are supposing here.

The household production technology is represented by a production function exhibiting constant returns to scale:

$$c^h = c\left(z^h, \lambda^h\right). \tag{2.1}$$

All households have the same preferences:

$$U^h = U\left(x^h, c^h, L^h\right). \tag{2.2}$$

The government observes incomes, not labour supplies or wages, and has at its disposal a general income tax, $T(y)$. The income tax schedule, in turn, determines disposable income $b = y - T(y)$. The choice of the income tax schedule will be presented equivalently as the choice of pairs of pre-tax and disposable income, one pair for each type of household, subject to self-selection. The government also sets linear commodity taxes, as we continue to assume that, for marketed commodities, the government only observes anonymous transactions. All marketed commodities are produced with effective labour as the only input and with linear technologies. Consumer prices are thus given by the producer prices (which we take to be constant and all equal to unity—see Chap. 1) plus linear indirect taxes/subsidies: the z-good has a consumer price $q_z = 1 + t_z$ while the x-good has a consumer price $q_x = 1 + t_x$.

2.1.1 The consumer's and the Government's Problems

As we saw in Chap. 1, one can usefully divide the consumer's problem in two steps. First, the household chooses its labour supply: this, given the presence of the income tax, is tantamount to choosing the disposable income. Second, the household chooses how to allocate such a disposable income and, in the present setup, also its total non-market hours among their possible uses. Taking the second step first, one can state that the consumer chooses x, z and λ so as to maximise

[2] Anderberg and Balestrino (2000), whose model provides the basis for the present section, actually have vectors of final consumption goods and inputs; here, we chose a simpler version for ease of exposition.

$$U\left(x^h, c\left(z^h, \lambda^h\right); 1 - l^h - \lambda^h\right) \text{ s.t. } q_x x^h + q_z z^h = b^h. \tag{2.3}$$

To save space and time, we skip the details of the derivation, which are pretty standard and follow the same steps as in Chap. 1, and simply write the indirect utility function with the government policy tools as arguments:

$$V^h = V\left(q_x, q_z, b^h, y^h; w^h\right), \tag{2.4}$$

where we used that $y = w(1 - L - \lambda)$. As before, we impose the single-crossing condition to make sure that type-2 agents always have a higher pre-tax and post-tax income than type-1 agents. In the first step, the household chooses its labour supply, or, equivalently, a (y, b) pair from the menu offered by the government. Since $V(\cdot)$ gives utility in terms of the policy variables, one can now describe how the government optimally selects the income tax as well as the commodity taxes.

Following Chap. 1 again, we study Pareto-efficient arrangements in which the planner maximizes one type's utility subject to the other type's utility being constant, and to the self-selection and revenue constraints; also, we treat the standard case in which the redistribution goes from the high- to the low-ability households; finally, the variables referring to the "mimicker" are distinguished by a hat.

The government's problem is thus to choose q_x, q_z, y and b so as to

$$\max V\left(q_x, q_z, b^2, y^2; w^2\right) \tag{2.5}$$

$$\text{s.t. } V\left(q_x, q_z, b^1, y^1; w^1\right) \geq \overline{V}; \tag{2.6}$$

$$V\left(q_x, q_z, b^2, y^2; w^2\right) \geq \hat{V}\left(q_x, q_z, b^2, y^2; w^1\right); \tag{2.7}$$

$$n^1\left(T\left(y^1\right) + t_x x^1 + t_z z^1\right) + n^2\left(T\left(y^2\right) + t_x x^2 + t_z z^2\right) = R. \tag{2.8}$$

2.2 The Tax Rules

We start by noting that the problem is formally identical to that presented in Chap. 1, apart from the added features that distinguish the present approach: (i) non-market hours differ from leisure, since the agents choose how to allocate their non-market hours to home-time and to leisure; (ii) the two commodities play two different roles, one being a final consumption good and the other being an input into home-production.

Hence, the standard results for the optimal income tax system apply. That is, in the presence of indirect taxation, we can confirm that the result shown in Edwards et al. (1994) is still valid: the low- (high-) ability households face a positive (zero) marginal effective income tax rate.

Focusing now on indirect taxes, it remains true that they are intended to deter mimicking behaviour by discouraging the use of those goods that are consumed by the mimicker more than her genuine type-1 counterpart. However, the fact that the mimicker works less than the type-1 agent (because she has a higher wage and the same income) does not necessarily imply that she will enjoy more leisure—non-working time is *not* the same as leisure. Hence, the link between taxation and complementarity with leisure is weakened.

As mentioned before, this has implications for the Atkinson-Stiglitz theorem. Once domestic production is brought into the picture, certain commodities will necessarily be related to the production process (i.e. to the share of non-working time allocated to home-production), either as inputs or as market substitutes.

In order to gain a clearer insight, we will employ several specialisations of the model, each designed to highlight a differerent issue. As already mentioned, these variants of the model are taken mainly from Anderberg and Balestrino (2000) and Balestrino et al. (2003).

2.2.1 *Taxing Input Goods*

In this section we will deal specifically with the question of the tax treatment of input goods *vis-a-vis* general consumption. In order to somehow "freeze" the role of leisure, we will assume additive separability in the following way:

$$U^h = f\left(x^h, c\left(z^h, \lambda^h\right)\right) + \varphi\left(1 - l^h - \lambda^h\right), \tag{2.9}$$

where f is increasing and quasi-concave in (x, c), φ is increasing and concave in its argument, and c is homogeneous of degree one. Given that the consumer's problem is well-behaved and that the mimicker has more non-market hours than does the type-1 agent, it follows that she will allocate more time to both leisure and household production.

It has already been established that the input good should be heavily taxed if the mimicker purchases it to a larger extent than the actual low-ability household. From the formulation of utility given above, one can understand that the complementarities in consumption and in household production will play a crucial role. Suppose for example that there is (i) a *high* degree of complementarity between z and λ in home-production and (ii) a *low* degree of complementarity between x and c in consumption: then, since the mimicker has a larger time input, she will also purchase large quantities of the input so that the household produced good will tendentially replace the general consumption good in her basket. In this scenario, the input good should be taxed *more* heavily than the final consumption good. Alternatively, suppose that there is (i) a *low* degree of complementarity between z and λ and (ii), a *high* degree of complementarity between x and c: then, the mimicker should substitute the time input for the input good in the home-production process and also purchase larger quantities of the final consumption good x, so as to accompany her larger production of c. In this scenario, the input should be taxed *less* heavily than the final consumption good.

Anderberg and Balestrino (2000) prove that this is true in a precise sense. They show the following (details in the original paper). Let η be the elasticity of substitution between the inputs to home-production, i.e. the input good and home-time; also, let ε be the elasticity of substitution between the two consumption goods: then, with constant returns to scale in household production (as assumed), incentive-compatible Pareto efficient taxation requires that the input good z is taxed more (less) heavily than final consumption x as long as $\eta < (>) \varepsilon$. Uniform commodity taxation is optimal if and only if $\eta = \varepsilon$. Thus, the role played by indirect taxation is not dependent on the relationship between the commodities and leisure: an input good should be taxed *more* heavily than general consumption as long as there is a high degree of complementarity in household production. Notice how the Atkinson-Stiglitz theorem fails to apply even if leisure is separable.

2.2.2 Taxing Market Substitutes

Let us consider now the tax treatment of goods that are close substitutes for goods and services produced in the household. As mentioned, Sandmo (1990) made an efficiency-based case in favour of tax concessions for these goods: in his model with identical individuals and linear taxes, such a lenient taxation helps to counteract the distortion towards household production that an income tax generates.

Let us see what happens in our model with two agent types and non-linear taxes, in which the government has also equity concerns. To begin with, let us take a simple model in which household production requires home-time only, there is a linear home-production technology, and a perfect substitute for the home-produced commodity exists. So, we have

$$c^h = a\lambda^h, \tag{2.10}$$

where a can be thought of as domestic ability (as opposed to market ability w) and is taken not to vary across agents; there are *two* marketed commodities, x and ε, where x represents now general consumption, whereas ε is the perfect substitute for c. The total consumption of the latter good will then be $g = \varepsilon + a\lambda$.

The agent's utility function would then be

$$U^h = U\left(x^h, g^h, 1 - l^h - \lambda^h\right). \tag{2.11}$$

This is a very specific but interesting case, again taken from Anderberg and Balestrino (2000), yielding particularly sharp results. We start from a situation in which only the income tax is in place.

To proceed, we need an assumption about the relative efficiencies in market- and household production. We take the case where $w^2 > w^1 > a$, so that no agent will ever engage in household production as long as the economy is in a *laissez-faire* (or indeed any other first-best) situation. However, this does not preclude positive household production under second-best taxation. Intuitively this may occur because, as we know, optimal non-linear income taxation involves, in the absence of indirect taxes, a positive marginal tax rate for the low-ability agents (to discourage mimicking). By lowering the net return on working hours, this might actually make household production worthwhile for these agents—for the high-ability one, instead, this will not happen, because their optimal income tax rate is zero.

Of course, the actual use of an inferior household production technology is what constitutes a distortionary impact in this setting: agents will tend to move away from market work towards non-market hours, as these generate consumption of g simply via the home-production of c, as opposed to purchasing the market substitute ε. Now, it is intuitively clear that, in order to counteract such distortion, the government's only possibility is to subsidise the market substitute (there are no inputs goods and home-time cannot be observed—just as in Sandmo's case).

This turns out indeed to be the optimal outcome of the taxation problem. Again, we only provide the intuition here and refer the reader to the original paper for the details. As we know, the non-linear income tax is the main instrument for re-distribution, while commodity taxation is aimed mainly at relaxing the self-selection constraint. Hence, commodity taxes are set high on commodities used in large amounts by a high-ability household when mimicking a low-ability household. The mimicker, however, has a relative abundance of non-market hours and is thereby prone to purchase *small* quantities of market substitutes; thus, the market substitutes should be taxed *lightly*.

2.2.3 Taxing Input Goods and Market Substitutes

Finally, we focus, like Sandmo (1990), on the taxation of a market substitute on the one hand and an input good on the other. Earlier, we noted that there is a case for taxing an input good heavily if there is a high degree of complementarity in home-production; also, we noted that there is a case for the lenient taxation of a market substitute for the household produced good. These observations can be combined to obtain the same policy prescription as Sandmo, namely that there typically will be a case for taxing the input more heavily than the market substitute. Thus, Sandmo's result continues to hold even in the present setting with differentiated households and non-linear taxes.

We can use the same utility function as above, but now we have $g = \varepsilon + c(z, \lambda)$, that is the home-production function is again a function of both time and an input good. As usual, the mimicker has more non-market hours to allocate; hence we would expect him to choose a larger time-input than the low-ability type. Assuming both (i) complementarity in home-production and (ii) that all goods are normal, we deduce that the mimicker buys more of the input z and less of the market substitute γ than the low-ability type. Moreover, z and y are naturally Hicksian substitutes. Suppose also that, as the price of x goes up, the consumer shift towards ε by buying more of the substitute y as well as the input z, i.e. that y and z are both Hicksian substitutes for x. The argument is then closed: the input good should be taxed heavily, whereas the market substitute should be taxed lightly.

2.2.4 *User Charges*

The result even extends to a model in which user charges can be levied on the time used to enjoy a public good. This case is an interesting one because it covers an instance in which one of the uses of time can be publicly observed and therefore it can be affected directly by the government. Adapting a formulation originally used by Anderberg et al. (2000), suppose that each agent's total time endowment can be devoted to labour l, leisure L and the consumption of a public good, s. The public good is denoted by G; there is also a private good x, which for simplicity does not require a time input. The public good and the time input are combined to provide a service $g(s, G)$—think of example as G as a museum, or as a streaming service over the internet, or even as a system of public roads.[3] The utility function is thus

$$U^h = U\left(x^h, g\left(s^h, G\right), L^h\right). \tag{2.12}$$

Both the utility function and the home-production function are strictly concave and increasing in their arguments. Production technologies for x and G are linear and use labour as the only input; production prices are thus fixed. It is immediate to see that this set-up is amenable to the same analysis, and the same results, as before. A Pareto-optimally chosen linear user charge t_y, to be defined alongside an optimal non-linear income tax, can be applied to the observable use of time for the production of the service g. Such a user charge will be positive as long as the mimicker devotes more time to the enjoyment of the public good than the true low-wage agent—still supposing that the redistribution goes in favour of the latter. Or, to put the result in a different language, a Pareto-optimal user charge is strictly positive as long as the time-input s is "normal" in available non-working hours $1 - l$. Moreover, the Atkinson-Stiglitz result fails to apply: even with weakly separable preferences ($U_{xL} = U_{gL} = 0$), it would still be true that a mimicker devotes a larger time-input to the production of the service than the actual low-wage agent. User charges, in this context, perform the same role as commodity taxes in the previous example, i.e. help relax the self-selection constraint.

[3] For all these situations, there is of course an obvious case for user chargers as an anti-congestion measure. The argument provided here is independent from these considerations.

2.2.5 Summary So Far

The current analysis supports, then, the general idea that, in the presence of domestic production, indirect taxation plays a similar role to that in the simpler model in which only leisure features as a use of non-working time, although with distinctly different features. This happens because the income tax (be that a simple linear tax or a more sophisticated non-linear tax) discourages work and so induces the agents to spend more time in household production: the distortionary impact can be at least partially offset by a well-tailored set of commodity taxes meant either to encourage the use of market substitutes of home-produced goods or to discourage the use of marketed inputs in the home-production process. Indeed, the direct manipulation of non-working time through policy instruments is not possible, in general, and therefore the governments must resort to this indirect route: when a direct impact on the time allocation is instead permitted by the circumstances, an immediate instrument such as a user charge for the publicly observable time used to produce a private good (a service, to be precise) can be employed. As mentioned, this is not dissimilar to what happens in the standard model, but it has the additional feature of being a more robust result. In fact, in the standard model, weak separability of commodities from labour is sufficient to exclude any role for indirect taxation in the presence of a non-linear income tax: this is no longer true in the present setting because certain marketed goods are naturally related to the home-produced ones.

The analysis so far has however been predicated on the assumption that while agents differ in terms of their market ability, they all have the same domestic ability. We now introduce the third characteristic of the model mentioned above, namely a differentiation of agents along two dimensions.

2.3 Redistributive Taxation in the Presence of Bi-dimensional Differences Among Households

Having discussed the role of indirect taxation in a model with home-production but with agents still differing only along one dimension, we would now like to enlarge the scope of our analysis by introducing bi-dimensional differences among households. In this new setting, we will try and understand the nature of the redistributive process and of the income tax as well as the impact that this has on indirect taxation.

To this end, we will base out analysis mostly on Balestrino et al. (2003). They argue that the role of differences in non-marketable skills in the definition of optimal policies is best understood in a model in which the home-produced good is *non-tradeable*, so that a perfect substitute is *not* available in the market. This would thus cover also the case in which the household is made of more than one person, so that we might include such things as love, companionship, or children in the list of domestically producible goods—clearly these are not tradeable goods nor they have perfect market substitutes. But, we might make a similar argument also for more ordinary goods, such as a meal cooked and eaten at home: certain market substitutes such as a meal at a pub or home-delivered are available but they are not perfect, as they may be of different quality (be that higher or lower) and also because the domestic production process may generate joint outputs that enter the utility function. We will build our model accordingly.

2.3.1 Home-Production of Non-tradeable Goods

The utility function that we employ, identical for both agents, is a variant of the one we used so far:

$$U^h = U\left(x^h, c^h\right), \tag{2.13}$$

with

$$c^h = c\left(z^h, \lambda^h; a^h\right). \tag{2.14}$$

So, we have that one of the goods from which the agent derives utility, c, is non-tradeable and domestically produced by the agent herself using her own time and the input good z purchased on the market as factors of production, while the other utility-yielding good, x, is directly purchased on the market. The main difference relative to the previous section is that we dispense with leisure: time alone does not yield utility (the time constraint is then $1 = l + \lambda$). This simplification is amply justified, we believe, by the analysis so far: the connection between market goods and leisure is not relevant for the definition of an optimal tax policy. Notice that the domestic ability parameter a re-appears here, and is now type-specific (also, its precise role is left unspecified for the moment). Pre-tax prices are fixed for the usual reasons; given what the government can observe, there are linear indirect taxes and the non-linear income tax. The household budget constraint, using the same notation as before, is therefore

$$q_x x^h + q_z z^h = y - T(y). \tag{2.15}$$

Following Cigno (1991, Chap. 2), let us notice the following asymmetry, which, as we shall see, is quite relevant for the definition of an optimal policy, especially, but not exclusively, relative to the direction of redistribution. Suppose that both λ and z are essential to production. Then, as a consequence, in *laissez-faire* an agent could not specialize completely in domestic production, because the input, z, needs to be bought on the market and this requires an income; on the other hand, assuming c is not essential in the utility function, an agent *could* in principle specialise entirely in market work (but, as we will see, it is not likely that she will do so). The asymmetry originates from the assumption that c has no perfect market substitute: if that were the case, a household could produce c exclusively, and then sell its excess production in order to buy the input, z, and the consumption good, x.

As mentioned, we assume now that households are differentiated by their market and domestic abilities. We have $w^1 < w^2$ as always; as for a, for now we simply state that, in general, $a^1 \neq a^2$.

Household choice can now be described in the usual way: the problem of choosing a second-best income tax schedule can be equivalently stated as that of determining two pairs of pre- and post-tax incomes $\left(y^h, b^h\right)$. The decision problem of the household is then solved in two steps. First, z is chosen so as to maximize

$$U^h = U\left(b^h - q_z z^h, c\left(z^h; 1-y^h/w^h, a^h\right)\right), \tag{2.16}$$

taking (y, b) as given. Second, the (y, b) pair (i.e., the labour supply, l) yielding the higher utility is chosen.

2.3.2 The Direction of Re-distribution

The analysis begins with a dicussion of the first-best case. This is useful to interpret the re-distribution process in the simplest possible way. In a first-best world, household characteristics would be known to the planner. We could then interpret the T in the budget constraint as a household-specific lump-sum tax/subsidy, and there would be no distortionary taxes. The household would choose x, z, λ to maximize $U(x, c(z, \lambda; a))$, subject to $x + z + w\lambda = w - T$ (recall that all producer prices equal unity). The indirect utility function, $V(T; w, a)$, follows in the usual way.

As is well know, there are two forces shaping an optimal tax structure, namely equity and efficiency. Normally, redistribution is driven by equity considerations, as we have seen so far—no matter whether home-production is accounted for or ignored (in this respect, the models employed in the first part of this chapter show no difference relative to the one employed in Chap. 1). Here, however, we argue that there is an efficiency argument for shaping the tax system in such a way that it favours those who have a comparative advantage in the home-production of non-tradeable goods: that is, we make a case based on efficiency consideration in order to justify redistribution. This is a radical departure from the usual way in which efficiency arguments are employed to justify the introduction of optimal taxes/susbidies, where they are usually related to such situations as, say, imperfect competition, public goods or externalities. In the latter case, for example, a tax might be imposed on polluting commodities in order to remedy the inefficiently high level of production that arises in a free market: that is, Pigouvian taxation. In this setting, a different reasoning applies.

In the Ricardian model of international trade, from which the concept of comparative advantage originates, technical coefficients are fixed; thus, comparative advantage is defined as the ratio of marginal costs or marginal productivities and is not affected by the quantity exchanged. We apply here the same logic, although the trade flow occurs between households, not nations, with the added complexity of variable coefficients, so that comparative advantage tends to disappear as the volume of trade increases.

As already mentioned, in our model a household with a comparative advantage in the production of the non tradeable good may be prevented by the budget constraint from specializing in this activity as far as allocative efficiency would require. In principle, complete specialisation in market work would instead be feasible. However, things are a bit more complicated than that.

To see this, let us begin by evaluating the comparative advantages in the *laissez-faire* economy. In our context, the natural measure of comparative advantage is the ratio between the marginal productivities of time at home and in the market, $(\partial c/\partial \lambda)/w$, where $(\partial c/\partial \lambda)$ is taken to be an increasing function of a. Notice first that the marginal productivity of home-time is not fixed, but decreasing: as already mentioned, this suggest that if an agent has a comparative advantage in domestic production, such an advantage will decline as she devotes more time to working at home. Moreover, we must consider that the ratio of productivities does not really reflect the incentives faced by the agents when taking their decision. Indeed, the marginal benefit for agent h of devoting one additional unit of time to home-production is given by the marginal productivity $(\partial c/\partial \lambda)$ times the marginal utility of c, and therefore equals $U_c(\partial c/\partial \lambda)$; similarly, the marginal benefit of devoting one additional unit of time to market work is given by the marginal productivity of labour times the marginal utility of income, that is $U_x w$. Since the marginal utilities (and, in one case, the marginal productivity as well) are decreasing, this implies that the hoseholds' incentives to pursue their comparative advantages are decreasing too. So, suppose that, for any two households h and k, we have $\left(\partial c^h/\partial \lambda^h\right)/w^h > \left(\partial c^k/\partial \lambda^k\right)/w^k$; while this certainly implies that household h has a comparative advantage in home production (correspondingly, k has a comparative advantage in market production), it must be remembered that, for the h-agent, the marginal benefit from devoting additional units of time to domestic work becomes increasingly smaller, as both U_c and $(\partial c/\partial \lambda)$ are decreasing, hence we do not expect in general that she will go so far as to fully specialize inside the home; the same is true for the k-agent when it comes to working in the market (U_x is decreasing too, although w is fixed). As a consequence, neither agent will achieve complete specialization: the typical solution for both of them will be an interior one, where the marginal benefits of the uses of time are equalized, $U_c(\partial c/\partial \lambda) = U_x w$—which is just the first order condition of the household's maximisation problem in *laissez-faire*.

We can interpret $U_c(\partial c/\partial \lambda)/w$ (i.e. the productivity ratio times the marginal utility of the domestically produced good) as a measure of comparative advantage in utility terms. Since, in *laissez-faire*, this equals the marginal utility of income, U_x, we can interpret differences in the latter as a signal that comparative advantages have not been fully exploited. If $U_x^h > U_x^k$, then household h has a comparative advantage in home-production, and k in market production.

We assume the following:

$$\partial U_x^h/\partial T > 0;\ \partial U_x^h/\partial w^h < 0;\ \partial U_x^h/\partial b^h > 0. \tag{2.17}$$

Since T is defined as a tax, the first assumption follows from the standard hypothesis that the marginal utility of income is decreasing in income. The second and third assumptions require a little more justification. Let us suppose, first, that individuals with high earning ability supply *more* labour than individuals with low earning ability (*no* backward-bending labour supply curve), and, second, that individuals with high domestic ability supply *less* labour than those with low domestic ability (a high value of b does *not* imply a strongly time-saving home-technology). Then, high-wagers with low domestic ability must have high incomes and, given diminishing marginal utility, low marginal utilities of income.

We have established that, at the free market equilibrium, comparative advantages may have not been fully exploited. This can be shown to affect the nature of redistributive policy. To see this, let us begin by framing the actions of the government in terms of the maximisation of a quasi-concave, Paretian social welfare function, $W = W(V^1, V^2)$. The government can achieve this by choosing T^1 and T^2 subject to $T^1 + T^2 = 0$ (no revenue requirement). This framing, while still guaranteeing that the chosen policy is Pareto-optimal (the social welfare function is Paretian, i.e. non-decreasing in its arguments, hence the socially optimal utility profile lies on the frontier), allows us to study how the chosen redistributive policy varies with the degree of inequality aversion embedded in the social welfare function and represented by the shape of its indifference curves (the more convex-to-the-origin they are, the more inequality-averse the government is).

In order to highlight the effects of the omparative advantages on redistribution in the starkest possible way, we shall refer to the polar cases of Benthamite and Rawlsian social welfare functions, whose indifference curves are straight lines and L-shaped, respectively. As is well known, the condition describing the optimal policy in the Benthamite case is $U_x^1(T^1, T^2) = U_x^2(T^1, T^2)$, whereas, in the Rawlsian case, it is true at the optimum that $V^1(T^1, T^2) = V^2(T^1, T^2)$.

Now recall that type-2 households have higher wage rate than type 1. Regarding the value of a, we can have $a^1 > a^2$ or viceversa—the case in which $a^1 = a^2$ is in fact the one with no-bidimensional differences.[4] Suppose then that $a^1 > a^2$: as we assumed that $\partial U_x^h/\partial w^h < 0$ and $\partial U_x^h/\partial b^h > 0$ (see above), it follows that $U_x^1(T^1, T^2) > U_x^2(T^1, T^2)$. We conclude that type-1 households should specialise in domestic production for efficiency reasons, but we know also that a complete specialization is prevented by the budget constraint. Now, the time allocation cannot be affected directly, but the planner can redistribute income in favor of low-wagers, so as to relax their budget constraint and allow them to specialize further in the activity in which they are relatively more able, ideally up to a point where comparative advantages are fully exploited (or, as close to such a point as possible). This, then,

---

[4] As such, it yields the same results as the standard case and it will not be treated here. Balestrino et al. (2003) notice however that the logic of comparative advantages is at work in this case too.

represents an argument for redistristribution in favour of type-1 households based on an efficiency consideration. However, equity may suggest that redistribution goes in the opposite direction: indeed, type-1 households, in this case, have also an absolute advantage in domestic production ($a^1 > a^2$), and therefore may have higher laissez-faire utility than type-2 if such an advantage is large enough to more than compensate the fact that the latter have a higher wage rate. What happens in this case in which the two motives for redistribution may collide?

If the government has Rawlsian preferences, the equity motive dominates. A Rawlsian planner will always re-distribute in favor of the household type with lower laissez-faire utility. In the case we just investigated anything is possible, so we cannot say whether type-1 or type-2 households will be the beneficiaries of the redistributive policy. But, if $a^1 < a^2$, type-2 households are necessarily better-off (we have not shown it formally, but it is easy to see that utility is increasing in both w and a), hence the planner will redistribute in favor of low-wagers.

If the government has Benthamite preferences, however, it is the efficiency motive that plays the dominant role. Assume that $a^1 > a^2$ and therefore $U_x^1(T^1, T^2) > U_x^2(T^1, T^2)$ as before. To achieve $U_x^1(T^1, T^2) = U_x^2(T^1, T^2)$, the planner must then set $T^1 = -T^2 < 0$, due to the fact the marginal utility of income is decreasing. Thus, redistribution goes towards the low-wagers, who have a comparative advantage in home-production, even when they are so good at it that they actually have higher *laissez-faire* utility than high-wagers. In the presence of an efficiency motive for re-distribution, then, a Benthamite planner will redistribute in a way that accentuates utility inequality. In the opposite case $(a^1 < a^2)$ it is impossible to say a priori which household type has the comparative advantage in home production: the direction of redistribution cannot be determined at this level of generality.

2.3.3 Optimal Second-Best Taxation

In a second-best setting, the government chooses the tax schedule (that is, the income tax and the indirect taxes) so as to maximize the social welfare function subject to the revenue constraint and to the self-selection constraints preventing each household type from mimicking the other (the analysis of the previous subsection applies when both self-selection constraints are slack, as we have in that case a first-best solution).

Normally, as we ourselves have done so far, the focus is on the case in which only one self-selection is binding, which is usually guaranteed by adopting the single-crossing condition (as shown in Chap. 1). In the standard model without home-production, we used the ''agent's monotonicity" (Seade, 1982) assumption ($-V_y/V_b$ is decreasing in the wage rate) to guarantee that only one self-selection constraint is binding. In the present model, however, agent monotonicity does not suffice to ensure single-crossing: we need to add assumptions on the domestic technology. There are a number of them: for example, the high-wager's indifference curves are everywhere flatter than those of the low-wager in the (b, y)-plane, if λ enters separably in the utility function and a does not affect the input mix in the production of c.[5]

Let us focus first on the income tax—suppose for a moment that indirect taxes are not applied. We know that only one self-selection constraint binds, due to the assumption of single-crossing; the direction of re-distribution determines which one. Now, without home-production and with households differing only in the wage rate, redistribution will be towards the low-earners as long as the social welfare function is quasi-concave, i.e. exihibits inequality adversion; the binding constraint will then be the one that prevents the former from mimicking the latter, as we have assumed to be the case so far. In the present model, however, the direction of redistribution depends on how the degree of inequality-aversion embedded in the social welfare function interacts with the bidimensional differentiation of the househols, as we saw in the analysis of the first best case. If redistribution is in favor of low-wage households, the marginal income tax rate on high-wage households will be zero, while the one on low-wage households will be non-zero, just as happens in the standard case. But, the opposite would be true if re-distribution were in favor of high-wage households. For example, consider the case in which $a^1 > a^2$ and type-1 households have higher *laissez-faire* utility. As we saw, the direction of redistribution here depends on the degree of inequality aversion embedded in the social welfare function. With Benthamite preferences, re-distribution is in favor of low-wagers, in which case the pattern of marginal tax rates is the usual one: zero for high-wagers, non-zero for low-wagers. With Ralwsian preferences, instead, the pattern is reversed: redistribution is in favor of high-wagers, whose marginal rate of income tax is therefore non-zero, while low-wagers have their time allocation undistorted. The intuition is of course the usual one: a non-zero marginal income tax rate is only useful inasmuch as it encourages the truthful revelation of type by making the policy package less attractive to the mimicker.

We now examine the possible advantage of introducing commodity taxation. First, this would enable us to repeat the analysis of the marginal income tax rates above, only it would apply to the marginal effective tax rates, as we have seen before. But a discussion of the sign of the indirect tax rates is more interesting. Without repeating the whole analysis, we know that if the only binding self-selection constraint is the one relating to high-wage households, a commodity should be *taxed* if a low-wage household buys *less* of that commodity than the high-wage mimicker, in order to to relax the self-selection constraint. However, if the binding self-selection constraint is the one relating to low-wage households, the optimal commodity tax is *positive* if the mimicker buys *more* than the mimicked.

Indirect taxation thus serves to alleviate the incentive problem associated with a non-linear income tax schedule, as usual. Now, in standard optimal tax models, differences between the consumption bundle of the mimicker and that of the mimicked arise only because of different wage rates. Here, however, there are two reasons why the use of a commodity may vary across types, since also domestic abilities

---

[5] Depending on the sign of the skill correlation, however, the steeper indifference curves could turn out to be those of the low-wagers (see Balestrino et al. 2003).

are different. Suppose, for instance, that $\partial z/\partial a > 0$ and z and λ are technological complements. In that case, the demand for c of the true low-wager is unambiguously lower than that of the mimicker if $w^1 < w^2$ and $a^1 < a^2$ (a low-wage person spends less time in domestic activities, and is less skilful at home, than the high-wage mimicker). That is no longer necessarily true when $a^1 > a^2$. Again, indirect taxes serve the same purpose as in the conventional model, but for different reasons: the simple rule that commodities that are, in some sense, complementary to leisure cannot be applied here, not even if we replace leisure with home-time.

Indeed, we can see this very clearly by replicating the setup for the Atkinson-Stiglitz theorem in our setting. Notice, first, that non-labour time, λ, plays a role analogous to that of leisure in the standard model. Suppose now that the utility function is weakly separable in x and c, and the domestic production function in λ and z: non-labour time, then, is weakly separable from commodities, just as leisure in the original formulation of the theorem. Hence, the demands for z and x do not depend on the time allocation, but only on the disposable income as well as, crucially, on the domestic skill parameter. Recall that non-market skills differ across household types, and suppose for example that $\partial z/\partial a > 0$ and $a^1 > a^2$: in that case, a high-wage mimicker will then buy less z than a low-wage household, while a low-wage mimicker will buy more z than a high-wage household. In general, therefore, commodity taxation may be desirable, alongside an optimally designed income tax. We have thus found that the Atkinson-Stiglitz theorem, even if it is re-formulated to account for a more general view of non-labour time, does not hold if we allow for differences in non-market ability (or, to put it differently, it requires, additionally, that variations in the domestic ability parameter do not affect the demand functions).

We have thus shown that indirect taxation retains a significant role, once we allow for bidimensional differences to enter the picture, in quite a general sense.

Chapter 3
Income Taxation with Two-Person Households

3.1 Introduction

In Chap. 1, we concluded in favour of a simple non-cooperative approach—whose roots can be traced back to Becker (1974)—relying on the standard Nash equilibrium concept in the spirit of Wolley (1988), Konrad and Lommerud (1995) and Anderberg and Balestrino (2007, 2011) as our main tool for describing the relationship within a couple. One of the most important reasons that we gave is that the non-cooperative approach captures immediately the fact that reasonable outcomes should be self-enforcing, since it is impossible to write binding contracts regulating intrafamily behaviour. At the same time, it is not an overly complicated approach and it is amenable to relatively straightforward analyses. In this chapter, we are going to study several issues concerning the taxation of couples under the assumption that the two partners behave non-cooperatively.

In particular, the present contribution takes the view that partners in a couple act non-cooperatively when taking decisions over *public household goods*, i.e. goods which are rivalrous and excludable across families, but are consumed jointly, without possibility of exclusion, within the family—see Konrad and Lommerud (1995). As a consequence, these household goods will be provided inefficiently. Care of the elderly or child-care are two examples that spring to mind: but, many commodities, ranging from house-cleaning services to children's education or preventive health-care, fit the definition of public household good.

The present chapter is largely based on Balestrino (2004). In turn, that contribution is closely related to the work of Konrad and Lommerud (1995), which also focuses on tax policy with non-cooperative families and contribution productivity differentials. However, while the two papers share a common background, they adopt different perspectives in their studies of tax policy. Balestrino (2004) explicitly emphasises optimal second-best taxation and tax reform issues, including the evergreen question of whether tax rates should be differentiated for primary and secondary earners (and of course we do the same here), while Konrad and Lommerud (1995) focus

A. Balestrino, *The Economics of Family Taxation*, Population Economics,
https://doi.org/10.1007/978-3-031-28170-9_3

on lump-sum redistribution within the family rather than redistribution via a distortionary tax system, and do not address the question of tax rate differentiation between spouses.[1]

In the standard view of optimal taxation and tax reform analyses in which the individual is taken to be the economically relevant unit, the usual focus is, as we saw in Chap. 1, on the problem of how to redistribute income from high-earners to low-earners while imposing a minimum of distortions on the economy. In that view, the equity-efficiency trade-off takes then a well-recognisable form in which redistribution can be advocated from an equity point of view, but can be argued against on efficiency grounds (depending on the shape of the social indifference curves, i.e. on the social preferences: utilitarian societies limit redistribution much more than rawlsian ones, for example). We already saw in Chap. 2 that the trade-off becomes however much less neat once we consider home-production, even if we stick to the approach in which a single agent (or a couple acting unitarily) is the main economic subject: for in that case, the presence of comparative advantages calls for redistribution on an efficiency, as opposed to equity, rationale. If we go further and replace the individual with a non-cooperative couple, our view of the trade-off needs to be revisited once more. Two things, indeed, spring to mind: first, there will be a need to correct for the inefficiency arising from the lack of cooperation, and this may provide a rationale for taxation which does not depend on the government's desire to redistribute income; second, given that the tax liabilities usually refer to individuals and not to families, there will be some redistribution taking place within economic units, i.e. from primary to secondary earners of the family—not only among units.

To be more precise, we study tax policy in an economy with intra-household inequality; thus, the government pursues both the aim of redistributing from high-earning to low-earning agents (which implies a redistribution within the family, as we just mentioned) and the aim of correcting inefficient behavior, while at the same time striving to minimise distortions. Since household goods are produced within the family using time, the government faces the problem of optimally distorting the agents' time allocations; this is typically an optimal direct taxation problem, but we adapt the same framework for a tax reform exercise. It is interesting to note that the presence of intra-household inequality due to a difference in wage rates implies a productivity differential in the contribution to the public good, and thus generates comparative advantages in market work vs. home work; the way in which the agents adjust their behavior to account for comparative advantages turns out to be crucial in determining the features of the optimal policy and the consequences of the tax reform.

It is important to clarify at the outset the driving forces behind the results presented here are the presence of (i) inefficiency,[2] and (ii) comparative advantages: indeed, were we to lose them, we would be back to a single agent setup! For example, if we

[1] Another important reference is Ihori (1996), whose model deals with international public goods but could be re-interpreted for household public goods; the focus of that paper is again on lump-sum redistribution between contributors, and, interestingly, on changing contribution productivities.

[2] On this, see also Anderberg and Balestrino (2007, 2011). The interaction between non-cooperative and bargaining models of the family is explored in Konrad and Lommerud (2000) and Chen and Wolley (2001).

had identical partners and assumed full altruism and full income pooling between them, then we would non really depart from the standard framework that we studied in Chap. 1—we would be, at most, in the territory traced in the first part of Chap. 2.

3.2 A Model of Household Choice

We begin by retaining our usual background: the economy is populated by two type of agents, differing only for their wage rates, and the total number of agents of each type is normalized to unity. We introduce however a new societal organisation: the agents live in two-person households. All the couples are identical, i.e. made of an agent 1 with wage w^1 and an agent 2 with wage $w^2 > w^1$. All agents have the same strictly convex preferences, defined over a private good, x, and a household good, g,

$$U^h = U\left(x^h, g\right), \text{ with } g = \lambda^h + \lambda^k, \tag{3.1}$$

where λ^h (λ^k) is home-time and $h, k = 1, 2$. The household public good is produced at home with a simple linear technology using the agents' own time, so that λ^h (λ^k) indicates the individual h's (k's) contribution to the aggregate provision of the household good. We also assumed that the time-inputs by the two partners are perfectly substitutable with each other; also, units are chosen in such a way that one unit of time gives one unit of the household public good. A good example for g in this case would be home-produced child-care. Finally, x and g are both normal goods. Let us stress, also, that agents are taken to be totally egoistic, as they only care about their own consumption. The formation of couples can be justified by noting that the present formulation is equivalent to assuming that there is a fixed utility gain from living together that can be ignored in modeling the agent's maximisation problem. Alternatively, we could have assumed that each agent maximises a weighted average of his and his partner's utilities: this would not have changed the basic results, as long as no full altruism is postulated (for in that case, it would be as if the couple were a single agent: this would completely eliminate the inefficiency but would also lay outside our interests).

Notice how the asymmetry between the agents motivates, as always, the optimal taxation analysis: indeed, because of this asymmetry, there is an equity-efficiency trade-off which can be addressed by tax policy; on top of that, the aforementioned asymmetry induces comparative advantages in the production of the household good vs. market production, which, as we know from Chap. 2, is going to have a huge impact on the nature of tax policy.

It is important to remember that while each individually contributed amount of home-time adds up to constitute a pure public good g *within* each household, g is a pure private good from an economy-wide perspective, i.e. *among* households. We use a second-best linear tax system, mainly for reasons of simplicity. So we take advantage of the assumption of constant returns to scale in production, as explained in Chap. 1: first, producer prices are normalized to unity by a suitable choice of measurement units; second, x is taken, without loss of generality, to be untaxed. Clearly, in this setup x can be equivalently thought of as consumption or net income; the budget constraint is

$$x^h = (1 - \tau)\, w^h l^h + T, \tag{3.2}$$

where τ is the marginal rate of income tax, T is a lump-sum subsidy and $l^h = 1 - \lambda^h$ is the labour supply—time endowment being normalized to unity ($h =, 1, 2$).

We assume that each person decides how to allocate his or her time between the two uses taking the other person's contribution to the household good as given: that is, agents have Cournot conjectures about the behavior of the other member of the household. Substituting (3.2) into (3.1), we can state the maximization problem as

$$\max_{\lambda} u^h = u\left((1 - \tau)\, w^h \left(1 - \lambda^h\right) + T, \lambda^h + \lambda^k\right). \tag{3.3}$$

This leads to the first order condition

$$-\, u_x^h (1 - \tau)\, w^h + u_g^h = 0. \tag{3.4}$$

$* * *$Solving (3.4) gives us the reaction functions $\lambda^h = f(\lambda^k; , T)$ and, symmetrically, $\lambda^k = f(\lambda^h; , T)$. A Nash-Cournot equilibrium is a pair $\left(\widehat{\lambda}^h, \widehat{\lambda}^k\right)$such that

$$\widehat{\lambda}^h = f\left(\widehat{\lambda}^k; , T\right); \quad \widehat{\lambda}^k = f\left(\widehat{\lambda}^h; , T\right). \tag{3.5}$$

We can now rely on two standard results from the literature on the private provision of public goods. First, Bergstrom et al. (1986, 1992) have shown that if preferences are strictly convex, as we have assumed to be the case, and both x and g are normal, as we also assumed, then the Nash-Cournot equilibrium exists and is unique. Second, non-cooperative behavior generates underprovision: both agents would be better-off if the provision level were increased, but since each partner does not acknowledge the fact that his or her contribution to the public good benefits the other partner, underprovision will prevail at the market equilibrium.

As we already noticed in Chap. 1, it is often more convenient to work with gross income $y = w(1 - \lambda)$ than with home-time λ. Using that $l = y/w$, indirect utility at the Nash-Cournot equilibrium can be written as

$$V^h = V(\tau, T) \equiv U\left((1 - \tau)\, y^h + T, 1 - y^h/w^h + 1 - y^k(\tau, T)/w^k\right), \quad h, k = 1, 2. \tag{3.6}$$

We then use the envelope theorem to obtain

$$\frac{\partial V^h}{\partial T} = U_x^h - \frac{U_g^h}{w^k}\frac{\partial \widehat{y}^k}{\partial T} = U_x^h\left(1 - (1 - \tau)\, w^h \frac{\partial \widehat{l}^k}{\partial T}\right); \tag{3.7}$$

$$\frac{\partial V^h}{\partial t} = -U_x^h \widehat{y}^h - \frac{U_g^h}{w^k}\frac{\partial \widehat{y}^k}{\partial t} = -U_x^h\left(\widehat{y}^h + (1 - \tau)\, w^h \frac{\partial \widehat{l}^k}{\partial t}\right), \tag{3.8}$$

and similarly for agent k. It has to be remarked that what is distinctive about the above derivatives is their inclusion of the effect of policy tools on the "externality" that each agent generates for the other by providing the public good non-cooperatively.

As a last element, we report the comparative statics at the Nash-Cournot equilibrium, which, provided that the labour-supply curve is not backward-bending, is

$$\frac{\partial \widehat{\eta}^h}{\partial T} < 0; \quad \frac{\partial \widehat{y}^h}{\partial T} < 0; \quad \frac{\partial \widehat{y}^h}{\partial t} < 0, \quad h = 1, 2. \tag{3.9}$$

where η is compensated gross income; the labour supply derivatives have, clearly, the same signs. Hence, both tax instruments (the poll-subsidy as well as the marginal tax rate) affect gross income (and labour supply) negatively.

3.3 Income Taxation

3.3.1 Comparative Advantages and Tax Policy

We now discuss what the assumptions we made on the productivity levels (inside home and on the market) imply for the existence of comparative advantages. These are customarily measured by the ratio between marginal productivities: in our setup, these would be w^h on the market and 1 at home. Given that we assumed that $w^h > w^k$, it follows that agent h has a comparative advantage in market work, while agent k has a comparative advantage in home-work. On the surface, this would seem to imply that the partners settle for a corner solution: indeed, the productivity ratio is independent of quantities, so one would expect that comparative advantages would be exploited to the maximum possible extent. However, it turns out that is not the case in general. To keep things simple, let us present the argument for the case of separable utility, leaving to the reader the minor adjustments needed to generalize the reasoning to any preference structure. Suppose then that

$$U\left(x^h, g\right) = f\left(x^h\right) + \varphi\left(g\right), \; h = 1, 2. \tag{3.10}$$

To begin with, we find that corner solutions are *not* the standard solutions in *laissez-faire:* the type 1-agent cannot completely specialize in home-work, otherwise he or she will have no private consumption; second, the type 2-agent could indeed fully specialize in market work and still enjoy the public good produced by the type 1-agent, but it is unlikely that he or she will actually want to do so. This is because the ratio of productivities does not really reflect the incentives that he or she faces when taking their decision. Indeed, each additional unit of time devoted to the production of g generates a marginal benefit for agent 1 which is given by the marginal productivity *times the marginal utility of* s, and therefore equals $U_g^1 \equiv \varphi'$; similarly, each additional unit of time devoted to market work generates a marginal benefit given by the marginal productivity *times the marginal utility of net income*, that is $w^1 U_x^1 \equiv w^1 f'$. Now, we know that marginal utilities are decreasing: therefore, the agents' incentives to pursue their comparative advantages are decreasing too. As a consequence, the 1-agent's receives increasingly smaller benefits from devoting additional units of time to market work, so that in general he or she cannot be expected to go so far as to fully specialize outside home.

Indeed, notice that the first order condition (3.4) could easily be rewritten, in this context, as $w^h f' = \varphi'$- with $\tau = 0$ because we are in *laissez-faire*. This already tells us that the typical outcome is that neither agent will achieve complete specialization: the normal solution for both of them will be an interior one, where the marginal benefits of the two alternative uses of time are equalized. To be precise, the same would be true in the presence of second best linear income taxation, such as the one assumed here: in that case, it would be true that even an agent fully employed at home would have some private consumption ($x^h = T$), but there is no reason to believe that this would change the outcome, since marginal incentives are not substantially affected: indeed, once we replace the gross wage rate w^h with the net wage rate $(1 - \tau)\, w^h$, the same analysis as above applies.

What we can say, in both cases, is that the tendency to specialize according to the comparative advantages will presumably have the effect of making the labour supply of the high-wage agent larger (or in any case not smaller) than that of the low-wage agent. So, we conclude that both in *laissez-faire* and under second-best taxation, the expected solution for the partners is an interior one, and high-wagers will work no less and earn more than low-wagers.

Actually, only if the social planner knew the agent's distinguishing characteristics (the wage rates), that is only if we were in in first-best, then a policy that allows a complete exploitation of comparative advantages would be possible. Suppose indeed that the government could use personalized lump-sum transfers and that the objective function is utilitarian (the sum of individual utilities). Then, at the optimum, the marginal utilities of net income would be equalized, $\Phi'\left(x^1\right) = \Phi'(x^2)$, and so would be private consumption levels. In this setup, then, the marginal benefit of working in the market would be *proportional* to the productivity by the same factor for both agents, which implies that it would be higher everywhere for the 2-agent ($w^2 f' > w^1 f'$ because $w^2 > w^1$), leading to a corner solution.

Hence, we conclude that, in this example, the high-wage partner will certainly work full-time in the market; on the other hand, the low-wage partner might work both at home and in the market or only at home. What is interesting to notice, however, is that while in either case the low-wage partner alone will provide the household good, his or her private consumption will be *the same* as that of the partner. The utilitarian planner, therefore, by redistributing in favour of the secondary earner to the point where marginal utilities are equalized eliminates the effects of the asymmetry in the possibility of pursuing the comparative advantages that existed in *laissez-faire*; also, the planner modifies the marginal incentives faced by the primary earner so as to allow a full exploitation of the comparative advantages. This latter point, of course, comes as no surprise: the utilitarian planner aims exclusively at maximizing the sum of utilities, or, to put it differently, it privileges efficiency above all things, and therefore the pursuing of comparative advantages is pushed to its limits (with other social objectives, instead, they may be left partly unexploited). It is worth noting that, in this particular instance, the utilitarian insistence on efficiency comes at no cost for equity, since consumption levels are equalised: this is however due to the assumption that preferences are the same across agents, and is by no means a general feature of the utilitarian optimum.

Extrapolating from the analysis of the first-best utilitarian outcome, we can argue that if we were to introduce a an income pooling assumption, then corner solutions would become normal in *laissez-faire* as well as in second-best. Suppose in fact that the agents engage in side-payments up to the point where their consumption levels become identical; then, they would actually behave exactly as the utilitarian planner, and obtain the same outcome. Unfortunately, however, income pooling is not an appealing assumption for at least two reasons. First, it does not fit well into a non-cooperative framework, where binding agreements are not possible and agents take the other agents' behaviour as given—that is do not engage in bargaining (actually, income pooling is usually ruled out also in bargaining models with strong gender specialization—see e.g. Pollak 2003 for a discussion); second, we have no clear empirical evidence in support of the hypothesis: Lundberg et al. (1997) find no evidence of income pooling, Barcena-Martin et al. (2020) suggest that is relatively common in Europe, but it is not clear whether it is full or partial pooling when present (and our argument above only works with full pooling), while Ponthieux (2013) finds inconsistent results that do non allow to ascertain whether income pooling is an established practice among European households or not.

Hence, from now on we will naturally focus on second-best equilibria in which both agents are at interior solutions, i.e. supply positive amounts of labour as well as home-time. Also, we will naturally take the type 1-agents to be secondary earners, and the type 2-agents primary earners.

3.3.2 Optimal Direct Taxation

In the presence of linear income taxation, revenue (in "per-couple" rather than *per capita* terms) is written

$$\tau\left(y^1 + y^2\right) - 2T = 0; \tag{3.11}$$

If we take the usual approach of finding the Pareto-optimal taxation scheme—say, maximizing the utility of the type-1 agent under the constraint of a fixed utility level for the type 2-agent—and then proceed along standard routes, using (3.7) and (3.8), and the Slutsky decomposition, we obtain a variant of the well-known optimal linear income tax rule,[3] which we already illustrated briefly in Chap. 1. To interpret this variant, we need to define the *generalized* net social marginal utility of income

[3] See e.g. Atkinson and Stiglitz (1981, Chap. 13).

$$\beta^1 = \frac{U_x^1}{\mu} + \tau \frac{\partial \widehat{y}^1}{\partial T} + \frac{U_x^2}{\mu} (1-\tau) w^2 \frac{\partial \widehat{y}^1}{\partial T}; \tag{3.12}$$

$$\beta^2 = \gamma \frac{U_x^2}{\mu} + \tau \frac{\partial \widehat{y}^2}{\partial T} + \frac{U_x^1}{\mu} (1-\tau) w^1 \frac{\partial \widehat{y}^2}{\partial T}. \tag{3.13}$$

This has also been already defined in Chap. 1; here we add the term "generalized" because the marginal utility of income includes not only the social value of the public funds μ ("social") and the effect on revenue ("net"), but also the effect on the other agent's welfare; any additional euro going to agent h makes him directly better-off (first term) but reduces tax revenue (second term) and affects negatively agent k's welfare by inducing a reduction in h's contribution to the household good. We need now two definitions: first, define a corrective term as

$$\varsigma = -\frac{1}{\mu \widehat{Y}} \sum_h U_x^h \widehat{\eta}^h e_y^h < 0, \quad h = 1, 2. \tag{3.14}$$

where $\widehat{Y}$ is aggregate gross income and $e_y < 0$ is the compensated elasticity of gross income w.r.t. net wage rate; this can be interpreted as representing the utility change due to the correction of household inefficiency; second, define

$$E_l = -\sum_h y^h e_l^h < 0, \quad h = 1, 2. \tag{3.15}$$

as (minus) the weighted average of the compensated labour supply elasticities w.r.t. the net wage rate, e_l.

The tax rule is then

$$\frac{\tau}{1-\tau} = \frac{cov(\beta, y) + \varsigma}{-E_l}. \tag{3.16}$$

The appearance of the tax rule is familiar, with the extra-term ς added to the ordinary *formula* holding in an economy with individuals and reported in Chap. 1. This is, as always, an implicit solution; we can however establish that normally, τ is included between 0 and 1. To see this, notice that since both E_l and ς are negative, then, for t to be between 0 and 1, it is sufficient, although not necessary, that $cov(\beta, y) \leq 0$. This latter condition is satisfied if β is non-increasing in w, that is if we assume that one extra-euro assigned to the secondary earner is seen as socially more valuable than one extra-euro assigned to the primary earner.[4]

In the standard framework with a unitary agent, the tax rules trade off two socially valuable objectives, the redistributive impact of taxation and the need to minimize the distortions imposed on the economy (equity vs. efficiency). Here, we add an important extra-dimension, namely the correction of the intrahousehold externality,

[4] The assumption that β is non-increasing in w is equivalent to an assumption that the income effects of taxation are very small; if that is the case, then the first term in the expression for β dominates the remaining terms and therefore, if the private marginal utility of income (U_x) is non-increasing in w, so is β.

whose importance stems from the assumption of a multi-person household whose member exhibit non-cooperative behavior as the relevant economic unity. The standard concerns here are represented as follows: if the elasticity term is large, it implies a large responsiveness of labour supply to taxation, then the planner should aim for a low tax rate so as to minimize distortions; since the covariance is negative, signalling that pre-tax income is distributed inequally in the economy, this calls for a high tax rate so as to foster redistribution from the primary to the secondary earner. The extra-element that we added here is that the corrective term suggests that there is an utility gain to be had from discouraging non-cooperative behavior, which in turn calls for a high tax rate so as to induce the agents to supply more home-time and therefore to increase the provision of the household good towards its efficient level. In other words, the income tax is, looked at from the perspective of the provision to the household good, a subsidy. Notice that, even if the covariance term were very small (even if there were very little pre-tax inequality), the optimal income tax rate would still be positive as long as the corrective term is strictly negative.

Assuming that economic units are made of more than one person and accounting for non-cooperative behavior within such economic units has thus helped us to establish that increasing the progressivity of the income tax (setting a large rate of income tax and a correspondingly large lump-sum subsidy) ameliorates welfare not only because more redistribution is performed, but also because the inefficiently low provision of the household good is remedied. Just as we saw in Chap. 2, although for somewhat different reasons, the consideration of comparative advantages within the household provides an additional reason for tax progressivity, quite independently from equity concerns.

3.4 Tax Reform

3.4.1 Alternative Income Tax Structures

In order to show that the discussion so far is not merely an "academic" one, but has also some relevance for empirical matters, we can apply our household choice model to the debate on the relative merits of alternative actual income tax structures—considering them, of course, at a rather high level of generality, not with respect to the more practical details

We may identify several different practices for taxing income. For example, it can be taxed *individually*, that is to say, the marginal tax rates may vary with individual income: in that case, within the same household the primary and secondary earners will face different marginal rates (this, for example, is the system used in most OECD countries). Alternatively, it can be taxed *jointly*, so that all the income-earners within a given household will face the same marginal tax rates (this, for example, is the system used in Germany and US). Also, individual taxation may be *progressive* and *anonymous*, in which case each individual income will face the same progressive rate schedule; or it may be, at least in principle, *selective,* in which case secondary earners within a household will face a separate rate schedule and lower tax rates. The "at least in principle" proviso is necessary because, on the one hand economic theory traditionally argues for a selective system, due to efficiency reasons: since the seminal contribution by Boskin and Sheshinski (1983) first made the claim, many authors have suggested that the secondary earner's income should be taxed less that the primary earner's one, because the former's labour supply is more elastic—selective taxation would therefore minimize distortions. On the other hand, though, there is no disputing the fact that the individual progressive anonymous system is the one prevalently used in practice (among others, Australia, Canada, Italy and UK). We will therefore focus our attention on this case.

One of the most common questions investigated in this field is whether a move toward a flat-rate tax in an individual progressive anonymous system is welfare-improving.[5] In our setup this would take the form of the following tax reform exercise: starting from a situation in which the primary earners face a higher tax rate, does a revenue-neutral reform that increases the rate paid by secondary and reduces that paid by primary earners improve welfare? For example, Apps and Rees (1999) have used a model of the family with efficient-decision making and household production of private goods to investigate this very question (see Chap. 1 for the various models of the family). They find that there are rather special and often empirically implausible conditions under which the losses incurred by the secondary earner can be compensated by the primary earner through intrahousehold trade, and conclude therefore that reforms towards a flat-rate income tax are unlikely to be welfare-improving. Ultimately then, the move is rejected on equity grounds—so this is not the same argument as the one in favour of selective tax rates, which is based, as we saw, on efficiency considerations.[6]

Here we perform the above exercise once again: is it socially convenient to move towards a flat-rate income tax? Is is welfare-improving? A key factor in our reply is our assumption that couples engage *non-cooperatively* in the home-production of a household *public* good. We cannot establish unambiguous results but we find that the move has, normally, one positive effect. Then, if this effect is large enough to offset other negative effects, the reform might be welfare-improving.

[5] Cyclically, the flat-rate income tax comes as the center of political debates in many countries. For examples, in Italy, it was championed by the right-wing coalition in the early 2000s during the electoral campaign, but never realised in practice once the coalition formed the government. Again, at the time of writing, mid-2022, the same coalition is actively championing the flat-rate income tax in pre-electoral times.

[6] Similar issues have been investigated, still within the unitary or collective model (or the bargaining one), by Kleven et al. (2009), Cremer et al. (2011, 2016) and Apps and Rees (2018).

3.4.2 Non Cooperative Time Allocation with Differentiated Tax Rates

We use the same model as before, in which a household good, public within the family but private in the economy as a whole, is domestically produced with a non-cooperative process. We suppose however that primary and secondary earners' incomes are now taxed at different rates, $\tau^k < \tau^h$. Household choice goes through the same steps as above, and, clearly, the results concerning the Nash equilibrium continue to hold. However, the fact that the tax rate is now agent-specific has important implications, because now at the Nash equilibrium, each agent's time allocation will depend also on the partner's tax rate. Indeed, now we define the Nash-Cournot equilibrium as a pair $(\widehat{s}^1, \widehat{s}^2)$ such that

$$\widehat{s}^1 = \varphi\left(\widehat{s}^2; t^1, t^2, T\right); \quad \widehat{s}^2 = \varphi\left(\widehat{s}^1; t^2, t^1, T\right). \tag{3.17}$$

A further consequence of having differentiated tax rates is that they alter the balance of comparative advantages: this will indeed play a crucial role in what follows. For example, notice that, relative to the *laissez-faire* situation, the introduction of differentiated tax rates implies that the secondary earner's comparative advantage in home-work will be reduced, given that he or she faces a lower tax rate than primary earner—the earnings differential has been reduced by the selective income tax, which is good for equity but not necessarily so for comparative advantages. As a consequence, in the present setup we do not expect comparative advantages to be fully exploited at the Nash equilibrium, rather we expect interior solutions to be the norm.

As we have already done many times before, we use gross income, rather than home-time, as the main variable. The comparative statics signs, barring special cases, are

$$\frac{\partial y^h}{\partial \tau^h} < 0; \quad \frac{\partial y^h}{\partial \tau^k} > 0, , \quad h = 1, 2. \tag{3.18}$$

To interpret the second effect it is sufficient to remember that if one of the two partners faces a higher marginal tax rate, he or she will reduce his or her labour supply (and therefore income) and hence increase his or her contribution to the production of the household; in turn, this will induce the other partner to adjust his or her time allocation accordingly, by increasing the labour supply (income) and reducing the time devoted to home-production. Indirect utility is

$$V^h = V\left(\tau^h, \tau^k, T\right) \equiv uU\left(\left(1-\tau^h\right) y^h + T, 1 - y^h/w^h + 1 - y^k\left(t^k, t^h, T\right)/w^k\right), \quad h = 1, 2. \tag{3.19}$$

The envelope theorem tells us that

$$\frac{\partial V^h}{\partial \tau^h} = -U_x^h \widehat{y}^h - \frac{U_g^h}{w^k} \frac{\partial \widehat{y}^k}{\partial \tau^h} = -U_x^h \widehat{y}^h - U_g^h \frac{\partial \widehat{l}^k}{\partial \tau^h} < 0; \tag{3.20}$$

$$\frac{\partial v^h}{\partial \tau^k} = -\frac{u_g^h}{w^k} \frac{\partial \widehat{y}^k}{\partial \tau^k} = -u_g^h \frac{\partial \widehat{l}^k}{\partial \tau^k} > 0, \quad h = 1, 2; \tag{3.21}$$

the signs follow from (3.18). Interestingly, each agent's utility is *increasing* in the tax rate faced by the other agent: when an agent faces a higher income tax rate he spends more time engaged in home-production, and this benefits the other partner, who enjoys a higher level of the public household good.

3.4.3 A Move Towards a Flat Rate System

Suppose then that we were to rise the tax rate on the secondary earner with a revenue-neutral reform $(d\tau^1, d\tau^2)$ where $d\tau^1 > 0$. Public revenue is written

$$R(\tau^1, \tau^2, T) \equiv \tau^1 y^1 + \tau^2 y^2 - 2T = 0; \tag{3.22}$$

to keep the reform neutral we have to ensure that

$$dR = \left(y^1 + \tau^1 \frac{\partial y^1}{\partial \tau^1} + \tau^2 \frac{\partial y^2}{\partial \tau^1}\right) dt^1 + \left(y^2 + \tau^2 \frac{\partial y^2}{\partial \tau^2} + \tau^1 \frac{\partial y^1}{\partial \tau^2}\right) dt^2 = 0; \tag{3.23}$$

it is important to emphasise that both terms in parentheses are presumably positive if we keep the elasticity of gross income w.r.t. the tax rate within its plausible range of values. Then, we get

$$\frac{d\tau^2}{d\tau^1} = -\frac{dR/dt^1}{dR/dt^2} = -\frac{\left(y^1 + \tau^1 \frac{\partial y^1}{\partial \tau^1} + \tau^2 \frac{\partial y^2}{\partial t^1}\right)}{\left(y^2 + \tau^2 \frac{\partial y^2}{\partial \tau^2} + \tau^1 \frac{\partial y^1}{\partial \tau^2}\right)} < 0. \tag{3.24}$$

This is indeed a trivial consequences of raising one of the marginal tax rates: if revenue is to stay constant, the other marginal tax rate must fall. Hence, revenue neutrality leads us in the direction of as a flat-rate tax system: the tax rate on the secondary earner goes up, while the one on the primary earner goes down.

It is relatively simple to show that we expect dt^2/dt^1 to be smaller than unity in absolute value. First, the high-earner provides a larger tax base; second, the direct effects ($\partial y^1/\partial \tau^1$ and $\partial y^2/\partial \tau^2$) should prevail on the cross-effects ($\partial y^2/\partial \tau^1$ and $\partial y^1/\partial \tau^2$): then, we conclude that a 1% increase in τ^1 can be made revenue-neutral by reducing τ^2 by less then 1%.

The effect on welfare is given by

$$\frac{dW}{d\tau^1} = \left(\underbrace{\frac{\partial v^1}{\partial \tau^1}}_{-} + \underbrace{\frac{\partial v^1}{\partial \tau^2}\frac{d\tau^2}{d\tau^1}}_{-} \right) + \left(\gamma \underbrace{\frac{\partial v^2}{\partial \tau^1}}_{+} + \gamma \underbrace{\frac{\partial v^2}{\partial \tau^2}\frac{d\tau^2}{d\tau^1}}_{+} \right). \tag{3.25}$$

The first term in each parenthesis indicate the *direct* variation in welfare for the two individuals: hadn't we included the household public good, we would have had only to compare those two terms. In the first parenthesis, we have the welfare loss for the secondary earner, due to the increase in his own tax rate; in the second parenthesis, the welfare gain for the primary earner, due to the reduction of her own tax rate. The usual test for checking whether the sort of tax reform considered here is welfare-improving relies on checking which of the two terms is larger in absolute value. What one expects, normally, is that the convergence of the two tax rates will optimally stop short of actually equalizing them, given that keeping a higher tax rate for the primary earner enhances redistribution.

Suppose however, for the sake of the argument, that the two direct terms offset each other with τ^1 still smaller than τ^2, i.e. that we have reached the minimum tax rate differential compatible with the equity requirements. It may be still true that a reform further reducing the differential is welfare-improving. To see this, consider the second term in each parenthesis, indicating the *indirect* variation in welfare for the two individuals: the loss incurred by the secondary earner due to the fall in the primary earner's tax rate and the benefit to the primary earner due to the increase in the secondary earner's tax rate. Notice that the term identifying the indirect effect on welfare is distinctive of our analysis and represents yet another effect of the presence of a non-cooperative production of a household good. Now, if the benefit to the primary earner is large enough to more than offset the loss incurred by the secondary earner, then a further move towards the flat rate system is welfare-improving.

What is the intuition behind this? We saw that, as long as income is not fully pooled, comparative advantages are not fully exploited at the second-best equilibrium; therefore, it is to be expected that a policy like a selective income tax, that hinders the pursuit of comparative advantages, could be improved upon. Indeed, it is easier for the couple to pursue their comparative advantages if the tax rate on the primary earner is reduced and the tax rate on the secondary earner is increased.

In other words, if we move towards a flat-rate income tax, then each partner benefits more from allocating his or her time in the direction which is consistent with the *laissez-faire* ranking of comparative advantages. The high-wager finds it more profitable to work in the market, and the low-wager finds it more profitable to work at home. So, while the reform's overall effect remains ambiguous, because the movement towards the flat-rate is clearly bad for equity, it is however fair to say that it becomes more likely to be welfare-improving if we account for non-cooperative home-production of a household good.

This is then a new way to look at the equity-efficiency trade-off: reducing the income tax rate for the primary earner and increasing that for the secondary earner might make the tax system less equitable, but it may benefit everybody by inducing time allocations more in line with comparative advantages.

3.5 Concluding Remarks

In this Chapter, we argued that taking a non-cooperative household, rather than an individual, as the economically relevant decision unit makes a difference for policy analysis. Besides the aforementioned assumption of non-cooperative behaviour, we also added an important element by identifying a category of goods, called household public goods, that are private across families but public within each family. Finally, we emphasised the role of comparative advantages.

We performed both an optimal tax analysis and a tax reform analysis. As far as the first is concerned, we found that the presence of household public goods calls for a high degree of progressivity. This is because the lack of cooperation induces a sub-optimal level of the private provision of household public goods; then, provided that the household good is produced at home with a highly time-intensive technology, a larger marginal rate of income tax acts as a larger marginal subsidy to home-time and therefore contributes to remedy the inefficiency. Interestingly, then, the optimal taxation analysis can be read as offering an economic rationale for progressivity based on efficiency arguments.

Also the tax reform analysis brings new insights. Traditionally, a reform away from a system in which primary and secondary earners are taxed at different rates towards a flat-rate system is viewed as undesirable, both in the standard framework and in the analysis based on the view of families as efficient units. This is mainly based on equity arguments, which remain valid within our approach. However, we emphasised that there is also an element pulling in the opposite direction: we found, indeed, that the reform gives the partners the right incentives to make their time allocations more consistent with the dictates of comparative advantages. Therefore the overall impact of a reform towards uniformity of the tax rates remains ambiguous, but as long as the advantage in terms of efficiency compensates the equity loss, it is possible that such a reform may be welfare-improving.

Indeed, the insights coming from the optimal tax and tax reform analyses can be combined to argue in favour of an income tax with a limited number of income brackets, or possibly, with a flat-rate combined with a tax allowance. Indeed, we saw that progressivity of the income tax is useful for reducing the disincentive to engage in the home-production of household goods arising from the non-cooperative behaviour of the couple, but at the same time it should be designed so as not to conflict with the correct pursuing of comparative advantages.

Chapter 4
Income Taxation and Public Spending with Two-Person Households

4.1 Introduction

In this Chapter we enlarge our view of government policy to consider not only taxation but also public spending, under the assumption that the significant economic unit is, as in the previous Chapter, a couple interacting non-cooperatively. To this end, we add the public provision of a private good to the government's toolbox. Relative to the previous Chapter, though, we change the model in one important respect, namely we rule out comparative advantages, so as to simplify the analysis and focus specifically on non-cooperative behaviour as the source of the inefficiency. The model is taken from Anderberg and Balestrino (2007, 2011); in those paper it is used to discuss several political economy issues, but we will adapt here to our discussion of Pareto-efficient policies (actually, we will consider a variant in which we look for *socially optimal* policies, which are Pareto-efficient but also allow for a discussion of the equity-efficiency trade-off).

One way of looking at the analysis that we will be undertaking is to think of it as an exploration into the relationship between family networks and the nature of the Welfare State. In traditional societies, the family would have been the main provider of services like, say, care of the elderly or child-care; more recently, however, they have become a matter of public policy (and increasingly so). One way to explain this would be to argue that these services are likely to be provided inefficiently in a *laissez-faire* economy, for the well-know reasons that have lead us to choose the non-cooperative family as the most sensible representation of the relevant economic unit: that is, because (i) enforceable contracts between family members cannot be written and (ii) learning through repeated interaction is not always possible (see Chap. 1). Indeed, it would made sense, from a collective point of view, to let the State take care of these services. Of course, this entails that the whole public structure is called into action: taxes must be raised, and not only to fund redistributional efforts, but also to correct inefficient behaviour and to fund other types of expenditures. However, different groups of individuals might be interested in different kind of policies: for example, low-income agents might prefer a policy package with a high

A. Balestrino, *The Economics of Family Taxation*, Population Economics,
https://doi.org/10.1007/978-3-031-28170-9_4

redistributive impact, even if that means that the inefficiency is only imperfectly remedied, whereas high-income agents would clearly prefer that the policies focus on fighting the inefficiencies rather than on addressing equity concerns. In turn, these tendencies may reflect themselves in different attitudes on the government part: some governments might be more interested in pursuing efficiency, other in pursuing equity.

So far, we have always assumed that in seeking to define a Pareto-efficient tax system, the government redistributes from the high-earners to the low-earners. Here, we take a broader view, in that we first establish a benchmark policy under the assumption that the government cares about efficiency as such, and basically ignores equity concerns; in that case, we find, within the limits of the model, that the government can achieve a first-best optimum with simple linear policy instruments. Then, we look at what happens if the government is concerned with redistribution towards the low-wagers. We see that in that case, the optimal policy gives more importance to equity-enhancing cash transfers (financed via a relatively high rate of income tax) than to efficiency-enhancing in-kind transfers. In other words, these governments prefer to under-correct the inefficiencies via the expenditure instrument, focusing on the redistributive role of the tax instruments. This suggest, by the way, that what we traditionally think of as *social* expenditures, in line with the standard interpretation of the Welfare State as a (collection of) redistributive device(s), might in fact be efficiency-enhancing tools—as such they would be favoured by governments which do not put much emphasis on redistribution.

4.2 Household Choice

We consider, just as in the previous Chapter, an economy where agents live in two-person households (couples) who behave non-cooperatively. Agents' preferences are defined over a marketed good x, which also acts as the *numeraire* and is untaxed (see the discussion in Chaps. 1 and 3) and a household public good g; as before, the latter is public within the household, but private across households.

The household public good is produced now using a slightly more complicated technology: it requires two inputs, one being a function of the time devoted by the two members of couple to household production, denoted g, the other being a publicly provided production factor, denoted d. As before, prime examples of the sort of household public good that we have in mind would be child care, children's education and health, care for the elderly and the disabled, etc. So, for example, a couple could provide care for a disabled child or an elderly parent by combining their own time with the services of a government carer.

The total time endowment for each agent is, as usual, unity: this can be used either for market work or for household production. The time endowment, in turn, is converted into effective units of labour, with one effective unit of labour producing either one unit of the input g or one unit of the marketed good x (or, one unit of the publicly provided input d). We further assume that agents have different productivities (they are equal in all other respects): so, when we label an agent as of type-w, we mean that the agent has w effective units of labour at his or her disposal. What we have then is an economy in which there are individuals of different productivities but for each agent the productivity is the same at home and in the market. To be precise, this is equivalent to assuming that an individual's productivity in the household and his/her productivity in the labour market are *proportional*, say w in the market and θw, where $\theta > 0$, at home. However, since since d is non-traded, we can normalise by setting $\theta = 1$. Notice that this formulation rules out comparative advantages across households; we discussed however the impact of comparative advantages at length in Chap. 3.

For our purposes, it turns out that the analysis is easier if we assume perfect positive assortative mating: hence, couples consist of agents with the same wage rate, and can therefore be identified by the latter. This is obviously just an analytically convenient exaggeration. Still, *positive* sorting, not necessarily perfect though, has been seen as theoretically appealing in Becker's early work (e.g. Becker 1981, Chap. 4); moreover, several empirical studies across the specter of the social science have supported the assumption and indeed argued that the evidence suggests that positive sorting has increased over the recent decades—see e.g. Mare (1991), Jargowsky (1996), Lou and Klohnen (2005), Robinson et al. (2017).

Following our practice so far, we assume for the purposes of the analysis in the present Chapter that there are (i) two agent types, 1 and 2, and (ii) n^h agents for each type, with $n^1 + n^2 = 1$; therefore, we have $n^h/2$ couples of each type. The couples are, as mentioned, identified by the wage rate w^h: as usual, $w^2 > w^1$.

We assume, just as in the previous Chapter, the partners' time-inputs are perfect substitutes,

$$g = (\lambda^h + \lambda^k)w, \tag{4.1}$$

where h is a typical agent and k is her partner, and where λ is, as always, the time endowment devoted to the domestic production process. The total time employed in home-production is then multiplied by the couple's productivity index, w, to obtain the total quantity of the domestically produced input. The product of the partners' effort, g, which we characterise as a household public good as defined so far, is then combined with the other input, d, which the government provides uniformly to all households as an in-kind transfer. This combination generates the service Γ,

$$\Gamma = \Gamma(d, g), \tag{4.2}$$

where $\Gamma(\cdot)$ is increasing and strictly concave. We adopt this general (or generic) formulation so as to cover various possibilities: e.g. the case in which d and g are complements and the one in which they are substitutes. It is however important to rule out corner solutions so as to keep the analysis manageable, so we do not allow g and d to be perfect substitutes; specifically, we take both g and d to be essential to production, that is $\Gamma(0, d) = \Gamma(g, 0) = 0$ for any d and g. Furthermore, we assume that utility for each agent is quasi-linear and ignore the distinction between the production of Γ and the utility that the household derive from it. So, we write

$$U^h = x^h + \Gamma(d, g) \tag{4.3}$$

(we could write $U = x + \Psi(\Gamma)$ where Ψ is a concave and increasing sub-utility function, but nothing of substance would change). The assumption of quasi-linear preferences is of course restrictive but it simplifies the analysis considerably and allows us, as we shall see, to identify a straightforward benchmark policy which satisfies the first-best conditions.

As common, and we have consistently assumed so far, the government only observes incomes, not wages or labour supplies. The typical budget constraint is

$$x^h = (1-\tau)^h (1-\lambda^h) + T, \tag{4.4}$$

where $1-\lambda^h$ is the labour supply, τ is the marginal income tax rate and T is a non-negative poll-subsidy. Substituting for x^h in the utility function (4.3) yields

$$U^h = (1-\tau)\, w^h(1-\lambda^h) + T + \Gamma\,(d, g)\,, \tag{4.5}$$

where g is given by (4.1). Each agent chooses λ^h for a given value of λ^k; we can then maximise w.r.t. λ, which leads to the first order condition (where the subscript indicates partial derivative)

$$\frac{\partial \Gamma}{\partial g} = (1-\tau)\,. \tag{4.6}$$

Solving this, we obtain the reaction functions

$$\lambda^h = f\left(\lambda^h; w^h, d, \tau\right); \boxed{2061}\, \lambda^k = f\left(\lambda^k; w^k, d, \tau\right). \tag{4.7}$$

Notice that the quasi-linearity assumption prevents us from including T among the arguments of the reaction function. Since each partner optimises by choosing her or his own time-input in the domestic production given the other partner's contribution, and, since, furthermore, the partners are identical, we clearly obtain exactly the same reaction function for both of them—just as we did in Chap. 3.

Again following what we did in Chap. 3, the fact that the agents are identical leads us naturally to focus on a symmetric equilibrium such that $\lambda^h = \lambda^k = \lambda$. Relying on the accurate characterisation of private provision equilibria provided by Bergstrom et al. (1986, 1992), it is immediate to see that such a symmetric Nash equilibrium exists.

Once again, to avoid the complications arising from the fact that the chosen time-input depends on the wage, we focus on pre-tax income, $y = w(1-\lambda)$ as the key endogenous variable. Clearly, since we have quasi-linear preferences, the pre-tax income y is linear in w. More particularly, we can show the following. Given that in the symmetric Nash equilibrium $g^h = 2w^h\lambda^h$, it then follows that, still at the Nash equilibrium, w and λ enter in the characterizing equation (4.6) only as a product, $w^h\lambda^h$. Hence, $w^h\lambda^h$ must be constant across household types, and therefore all agents, irrespectively of type, contribute the same value $w^h\lambda^h$ to the domestically produced input g. This in turn implies that pre-tax income can be written in an additive form,

$$y^h(w, \tau, g) = w^h - \omega(\tau, d), h = 1, 2, \tag{4.8}$$

where $\omega(\tau, d) = w^h \lambda^h$ is the (constant-across-households) contribution to the input g per agent. This has important consequence for the comparative statics: in fact, agents' pretax income react to policy in the same way:

$$\frac{\partial y^h}{\partial \tau} = -\frac{\partial \omega}{\partial \tau} < 0; \tag{4.9}$$

$$\frac{\partial y^h}{\partial d} = -\frac{\partial \omega}{\partial d} < (>)\ 0 \text{ if } g \text{ and } d \text{ are complements (substitutes)}, h = 1, 2. \tag{4.10}$$

As we can see, gross income decreases, as expected, when the tax rate τ increases; also, it can either increase or decrease when the publicly provided input d increases, depending on whether the latter is a complement to or substitute for household production g.

Finally, we identify the indirect utility function as

$$V^h = V(\tau, T, d) = (1 - \tau)\, y^h + T + \Gamma(d, 2\omega(\tau, d)); \tag{4.11}$$

the derivatives with respect to the policy instruments are:

$$\frac{\partial v^h}{\partial \tau} = -y^h + 2\frac{\partial \Gamma}{\partial g}\frac{\partial \omega}{\partial \tau}; \tag{4.12}$$

$$\frac{\partial v}{\partial T} = 1 > 0; \tag{4.13}$$

$$\frac{\partial v}{\partial d} = \frac{\partial \Gamma}{\partial d} + 2\frac{\partial \Gamma}{\partial g}\frac{\partial \omega}{\partial d}. \tag{4.14}$$

Note that the agent's type, i.e. his or her wage rate/productivity w does not appear directly as an argument in (4.14): in the symmetric Nash equilibrium, $\Gamma = \Gamma(g, 2\omega(\tau, d))$, which does not depend on w. Note also that (4.14) is positive if g and d are complements, and cannot be signed otherwise; finally, (4.12) cannot be signed. The ambiguity of the effects depend on there being two distinct elements in the impact of a variation of either τ or d: in addition to the usual direct impact on utility there is a further impact coming from the change in the Nash equilibrium.

4.3 Optimal Policy I: Efficiency

In order to characterize the optimal policy, we have to introduce a government budget constraint. The latter can be written as

$$\tau\left(n^1y^1+n^2y^2\right)-T-d/2=0 \text{ or } \tau\overline{y}-T-d/2=\tau(\overline{w}-2\omega)-T-d/2=0, \tag{4.15}$$

where the upper bar denotes an average value. Rather than trying to identify the Pareto-efficient tax system as we have done so far, in this Chapter we look at *optimal* policies, in the sense that they satisfy a social welfare objective. As we already mentioned, however, we will be using Paretian social welfare functions, which are defined over individual utilities and are non-decreasing in all their arguments: hence, the socially optimal policies will also be Pareto-efficient.

We begin with a utilitarian social welfare function, whereby social welfare is given by the sum of individual utilities. As is well-known, an utilitarian social welfare objective means that only efficiency is pursued—equity is irrelevant. We have

$$\begin{aligned} W &= n^1V^1+n^2V^2=(1-\tau)\overline{y}+T+\Gamma(d,2\omega)=(1-\tau)(\overline{w}-\omega) \\ &\quad +T+\Gamma(d,2\omega). \end{aligned} \tag{4.16}$$

The FOCs are

$$\frac{\partial W}{\partial \tau}=-\overline{y}+2\frac{\partial\Gamma}{\partial g}\frac{\partial\omega}{\partial\tau}+\mu(\overline{y}-\tau 2\frac{\partial\omega}{\partial\tau})=0; \tag{4.17}$$

$$\frac{\partial W}{\partial T}=1+\mu\,(-1)=0; \tag{4.18}$$

$$\frac{\partial W}{\partial d}=\frac{\partial\Gamma}{\partial d}+2\frac{\partial\Gamma}{\partial g}\frac{\partial\omega}{\partial d}+\mu(-\tau 2\frac{\partial\overline{\omega}}{\partial d}-\frac{1}{2})=0. \tag{4.19}$$

Simplifying, we have

$$(\mu-1)\,\overline{y}+\left(\frac{\partial\Gamma}{\partial g}-\mu\tau\right)2\frac{\partial\omega}{\partial\tau}=0; \tag{4.20}$$

$$\mu=1; \tag{4.21}$$

$$\frac{\partial\Gamma}{\partial d}+\left(\frac{\partial\Gamma}{\partial g}-\mu\tau\right)2\frac{\partial\omega}{\partial d}=\mu/2. \tag{4.22}$$

Using now 4.21 and (4.6) we obtain

$$((1-\tau)-\tau)2\frac{\partial\omega}{\partial\tau}=0; \tag{4.23}$$

$$\frac{\partial\Gamma}{\partial d}+((1-\tau)-\tau)\,2\frac{\partial\omega}{\partial d}=1/2, \tag{4.24}$$

that is

$$(1-\tau)-\tau=0 \text{ or } \tau=1/2;\; 2\frac{\partial\Gamma}{\partial d}=1. \tag{4.25}$$

Interestingly, then, the optimal utilitarian policy can actually reach the first-best optimum: the condition ruling the optimal supply of the publicly provided input is actually the Samuelson condition (the sum of the marginal benefits equal the marginal cost). The same condition holds for g as well, since using $\tau = 1/2$, we can write (4.6) as

$$2\frac{\partial \Gamma}{\partial g} = 1. \tag{4.26}$$

Notice that, clearly, the Samuelson conditions do not hold at the laissez-faire equilibrium, in which (4.6) becomes $\partial \Gamma / \partial g = 1$ (this is because in the absence of policy, the agents' non-cooperative behaviour determines an inefficient outcome). However, due to quasi-linearity and the ensuing characteristic that g and d are constant across household, a simple linear taxation system is capable of achieving the Pareto optimum when the social objective is utilitarian, i.e. efficiency-focused, in nature. Hence, in this particular instance, the tax remedies the inefficiency, acting as a "corrective" instrument. This efficiency-focused policy constitutes an interesting benchmark against which a more equity-oriented policy can be evaluated.

4.4 Optimal Policy II: Equity

The pursuit of efficiency as the government's sole objective has been ensured by the adoption of a utilitarian social welfare function. Suppose now that the government adopts a generalised utilitarian social welfare function in which individual utilities do not enter the social welfare function as such, but are multiplied by a so-called "welfare weight" ν^h:

$$\begin{aligned} W = \nu^1 n^1 V^1 + \nu^2 n^2 V^2 = (1-\tau)\widehat{y} + T + \Gamma(d, 2\omega) = (1-\tau)(\widehat{w} - \omega) \\ + T + \Gamma(d, 2\omega) \end{aligned} \tag{4.27}$$

where the hat denotes a (weighted) average value. Choosing the welfare weights appropriately, we may ensure that $\nu^1 n^1 + \nu^2 n^2 = 1$, but in general the "upper bar values" in (4.16) differ from the "hat values" here (unless of course $\nu^1 = \nu^2 = 1$). If $\nu^1 > \nu^2$, then the social objective will give relatively more weight to the utility of the low-earners—we take this to be the case, in line with what he have done so far (but the opposite case can be treated symmetrically).

If we go through the same steps as above to find the optimal policy, using however the new objective function of the government, we find the following:

$$t = \frac{1}{2} + \frac{(\overline{w} - \widehat{w})}{2\frac{\partial \omega}{\partial \tau}}; \quad 2\frac{\partial \Gamma}{\partial d} = 1 - (1 - 2\tau)\, 2\frac{\partial \omega}{\partial d}, \tag{4.28}$$

where we recall that $\partial \omega / \partial \tau > 0$ since a higher tax rate encourages household production. (Recall also that ω is type-independent). Clearly, these conditions collapse to

(4.25) when $\nu^1 = \nu^2 = 1$, i.e. when the generalised utilitarian social welfare function becomes utilitarian *tout court*, for then $\overline{w} = \widehat{w}$.

Thus, the optimal tax rate is the sum of two elements, capturing respectively efficiency and redistribution concerns. The first term is the corrective term; as we know, at $\tau = 1/2$, the Nash equilibrium private contributions satisfy the Pareto efficiency rule $2(\partial\Gamma/\partial d) = 2(\partial\Gamma/\partial g) = 1$, therefore the inefficiency associated with the non-cooperative behaviour of the household members is remedied. The second term represents the redistributive gain/loss; it is proportional to the difference between the weighed mean wage and simple mean wage, and it is positive if the former is less than the latter and negative otherwise. In other words, it is positive if society gives more weight to the low-income agents than to the high-income ones and negative otherwise. The higher is the equity concern, the higher is the tax rate—i.e. the more progressive is the income tax, as a higher tax rate implies a larger poll-subsidy. However, there is a distortionary element implicit in the redistributive component of the tax, and this is reflected in the appearance of a measure of the impact of taxation on household production or income, $2\,(\partial\omega/\partial\tau) = -2\,(\partial y/\partial\tau)$; intuitively, the more responsive is home-production (or equivalently income) to taxation, the less will the optimal tax deviate from the corrective tax $\tau = 1/2$. The message is straightforward: no matter what the societal objective is, it is always acknowledged that an income tax rate is useful for correcting the inefficiency stemming from household time being a public good and agents behaving non-cooperatively, but societies which give more prominence to the interests of the high-wagers prefer a tax rate *below* the corrective level in order to avoid too much redistribution, whereas societies which give more prominence to the interests of the low-wage agents prefer a tax rate *above* the corrective level to generate redistribution. If a society is solely concerned with efficiency, i.e. aims at the utilitarian optimum, it will opt to set the tax rate at exactly the corrective level.

As for the characterization of the optimal in-kind provision, it is useful to compare it with the Pareto efficiency condition $2(\partial\Gamma/\partial d) = 1$. As we said repeatedly, this condition holds under a utilitarian social planner which is not interested in the redistributive impact of income taxation and hence chooses a policy solely based on efficiency considerations. The interesting question, however, is there a reason why a government, even if it adopts a generalised utilitarian objective and is therefore interested in redistribution, would want to deviate from efficiency as far as public provision is concerned? In fact, one would expect that although societies with different objectives would have different attitudes concerning the extent of redistribution, and hence on the financing of g, they would all agree on g being provided at the Pareto efficient level. However, this turns out not to be generally true.

To see this notice that the second condition in (4.28) does not directly contain the weighed averaged value $\widehat{w}$. This implies that the condition defines a single locus in (τ, d)-space along which the optimal policies for all the generalised utilitarian social welfare function will be located. We can then study this locus to check how the optimal d varies with the optimal τ. Thus, we let d be an implicit function of τ; totally differentiating with respect to τ and solving for $d'(\tau)$ we obtain, after some manipulations,

$$d'(\tau) = \frac{-(1-2\tau)\frac{\partial\omega}{\partial\tau\partial d}}{\left(\frac{\partial\Gamma}{\partial g\partial g} - \left(\frac{\partial\Gamma}{\partial g\partial d}\right)^2 / \frac{\partial\Gamma}{\partial g\partial g}\right) + (1-2\tau)\frac{\partial\omega}{\partial d\partial d}}, \tag{4.29}$$

where the first term in parenthesis below the line is negative by concavity of Γ; actually, the entire denominator is negative by the second order condition of the agent's maximisation problem inherent in the Nash equilibrium. From (4.29) we see then that the sign of $d'(\tau)$ depends on whether τ is smaller or larger than $1/2$ and, importantly, on the sign of $\partial\omega/\partial\tau\partial d$ (which is unfortunately hard to determine, as it involves the third derivatives of Γ). Notice that if $\partial\omega/\partial\tau\partial d = 0$, then it would be true that at all generalised utilitarian social optima the Samuelson conditions hold for the household production inputs.

This actually explains why the condition deviates from the efficient one in general. Indeed, the term $\partial\omega/\partial\tau\partial d$ captures the extent to which the policy instruments τ and g interact between themselves: when it equals zero there is no interaction, but when it differs from zero, it is instead possible to use one of the two instruments to counteract the distortionary effect of the other. To see this, consider that when $\partial\omega/\partial\tau\partial d \neq 0$, changes in d alter the responsiveness of the agents' time allocations to taxation; therefore, by under- or overproviding d the government can reduce the extent to which $\tau \neq 1/2$ distorts the time-allocation. At least, this is the theory: in practice, it seems unlikely that the counter-distortionary impact might be so large to induce a significant deviation from the first-best level of d. Hence, we take $\partial\omega/\partial\tau\partial d = 0$ to be our reference case.

We can thus draw a straightforward conclusion concerning the optimal mix of public expenditure. If low-wagers enjoy a greater welfare weight than high-wagers, at the optimum we would have a relatively high τ and, correspondingly, relatively large income tax revenue, but the same level of public provision d (and hence the same total expenditure on d) than in the opposite case. Therefore, it follows that at the social optimum, there will be an expenditure *mix* biased towards the cash transfer, whereas in the opposite case relatively more resources would be allotted to the in-kind transfer.

That is, a concern for equity implies that the government should direct its resources not towards remedying the inefficiency in home-production but towards reducing income inequality: it should set the tax rate above the corrective level in order to raise funds for redistribution. On the other hand, if the government is not very concerned with redistribution because high-wager enjoy a greater welfare weight than low-wagers, at the optimum there will be low tax rates (below the corrective level) and low cash transfers while in-kind transfers will constitute a relatively important item of expenditure. This implies that, rather than using taxes, the government may remedy the inefficiencies using the expenditure instrument; however, this will have the effect to reduce the extent of redistribution. This highlights yet another way in which representing a non-cooperative couple as the relevant economic unit impacts our understanding of the effects of government policy.

Chapter 5
The Fiscal Treatment of Family Size: An Overview

5.1 Introduction

There is general consensus, among the populace at large and actually also among the majority of social scientists, that large families should be subsidised. Indeed, many governments share the view that children should be a tax asset to their parents and endeavour to make them so in practice, using per-child grants and/or income tax allowances related to family size (sometimes, less immediately by just as efficaciously, governments also implement a favourable tax treatment for children goods, such as reduced VAT rates for baby-food or clothes). This could be easily justified in a number of ways: children might be seen as generating positive externalities or as a sort of merit good or as an instrument to keep the PAYG pension system up and running. But, in line with the theme of the present book, we will focus our attention on the question whether a welfare-maximising government should devise the optimal second-best tax system in such a way that children are subsidised. The above-mentioned reasons rest on a different argument: basically, that society values children more than individuals, that governments are aware of this and therefore subsidise large families. There is no intention, here, to dispute those views: we just pursue a different line of inquiry, and in order to focus on our issue we restrict our field by assuming that the economy is second-best only inasmuch as distortionary taxation is used (so, no externalities are involved), that the government values children exactly as their parents do (so, no merit goods argument is invoked), and that the model is static (so, no pension system is active). In this sense, our conclusion are limited: we will assess the opportunity of subsidising family size (or not, as the case may be) from a specific viewpoint: no matter what we conclude, other arguments for or against retain their validity.[1]

[1] An exception must be made, however, for arguments based on equivalence scales. As we emphasised in Chap. 1, once fertility is taken to be endogenous and children are taken to be valuable to their parents, as we will do here, there is no way to savage the equivalence scales framework, that only works under the (implausible) assumptions that the number of children is given exogenously and that children only represent a cost for their parents.

A. Balestrino, *The Economics of Family Taxation*, Population Economics,
https://doi.org/10.1007/978-3-031-28170-9_5

In order to accomplish our task, we adopt a model similar to the one employed in Chaps. 2 and 3. We assume therefore the existence of a single parent, or that the parents act unitarily, rather than as a non-cooperative couple. Fertility is taken to be endogenous. What they produce however, is not a good or a service, but children: to be more precise, we assume that parents care for the quantity and the quality (of life) of their offspring. To be precise, the model we employ here belongs to the stream of work which deals with the home-production of *non-tradeable* goods (for which it makes little sense to talk of market substitutes—see Chap. 2), although with a crucial difference because children, unlike other non-tradeable home-produced goods, are observable and therefore taxable. Indeed, we then proceed to investigate the conditions under which a favourable tax treatment of family size is socially desirable. We cast our arguments prevalently in terms of the impact of taxation on quantities, rather than on consumer prices. We have already noticed (Chap. 1) that tax rates (and therefore consumer prices) are only determined up to a constant, so that statements concerning the absolute level of taxation cannot be made; to evaluate the effects of taxation, we have to identify the direction in which demands are distorted.

We also argue that the desirability of subsidising family size is critically sensitive to the form of the tax system. Following Balestrino (2001) and (partly) Balestrino et al. (2002), we cover all the possible tax regimes, thereby offering a comprehensive overview of the optimal taxation of family size. We start from the relatively obvious (but not always exploited in tax theory) observation that, since raising children and earning an income are the activities that absorb most of a person's time and energy, at least before retirement, they should *both* be carefully monitored for the purpose of devising a well-functioning tax system. In most contributions to tax theory, included the ones in this volume, income is taken to be observable; one should not forget, then, that the number of children is in fact easy to observe for the fiscal authority,[2] and therefore that reproductive behaviour conveys a great deal of information about a person's (fiscally relevant) characteristics.

First, we set up a benchmark by sketching a first-best policy and efficiency-oriented second-best taxes; then we move to redistributive second-best taxation, that represents our main interest. We start by focusing on a linear tax system and then on a mixed tax system, which is the one we have used more often than others in the previous Chapters. In the mixed tax system, the income tax, being non-linear, becomes the main instrument for redistribution, and the role of non-income taxes is mostly that of increasing the efficiency of the fiscal structure by discouraging false representations of preferences—as we already know from our previous Chapters. In the linear tax system, instead, non-income taxes play a substantial redistributive role; the redistributive impact of the linear income tax is somewhat limited, and it has to be supplemented by the other policy instruments.

[2] One of the primary functions of the State is, at least in relatively recent times, the recording of births and deaths, and of the composition of families. From the point of view of fiscal policy, the cost of performing such a function is given, and the marginal cost of retrieving this information for the purpose of tax design may be reasonably assumed to be negligible.

5.2 A Model of Family Choice

Once again, consider an economy inhabited by two groups of households, identified by their market ability, which is as usual normalised to equal the wage rate, w^h, $h = 1, 2$. As always, $w^2 > w^1$, that is the members of group 2 have higher ability. There are n^h households in each group, and population size is normalised to unity. Preferences are identical. Each household comprises two categories of individuals, parents and children. Parents act unitarily, as if they were just one person: this entity consumes x units of an adult consumption good, and has a "quantity" N of children. All children are identical; their "quality" (of life)[3] Q is a function of a children-specific good z and home-time λ.[4] It seems to be realistic to assume that, in order to guarantee the survival of a child, minimum levels of z and λ must be achieved. We use an underbar to denote these levels: $\underline{z}$ and $\underline{\lambda}$. Also, we set the scale of Q so as to have $Q(\underline{z}, \underline{h}) = 0$; finally, the function Q is homogeneous of degree one (i.e. there are constant returns to scale) in $(z - \underline{z}, \lambda - \underline{\lambda})$. We can then write parental utility as

$$U^h = U\left(x^h, Q\left(z^h, \lambda^h\right), N^h\right). \tag{5.1}$$

As always, production is linear, and labour is the only input: all producer prices are normalised to unity. Consumer prices are q_x and q_z for x and z, respectively. The list of tax instruments includes a lump-sum transfer T, a marginal rate of income tax τ, commodity taxes $t_x > 0$ and $t_z > 0$ (or subsidies, $t_x < 0$ and $t_z < 0$) and a child benefit, $B < 0$ (or tax, $B > 0$).

The distinctive trait of the linear tax system is that *all* tax rates are uniform across types; this may happen for example due to restrictions imposed by administrative costs. A mixed tax system includes instead, as we know, a non-linear income tax and linear commodity taxes. As for the child benefit, it is natural to assume that the fertility level can be observed in a non-anonymous way: the government clearly knows how many children each household has. As a consequence, children can be taxed non-linearly.

In order to make the comparison with the linear tax system easier, we abandon the practice followed so far of representing the non-linear tax system as if the objects of choice for the policy maker were directly the (net income, gross income)-pairs with the agents selecting the preferred pair; instead, we extend the approach originally developed by Nava et al. (1996) and represent the resulting tax system using income-contingent, piece-wise linear tax rates for the non-linear taxes, i.e. by making τ,

[3] The terms "quantity" and "quality" of children come from the Beckerian tradition. There are, in general, two ways to think about Q. If we strictly follow Becker (1981), it may be viewed as a composite consumption good, destined to the children of each specific household, produced at home by the child's parents using their own time as well as marketed child-specific commodities. Alternatively, if we follow Cigno (1991), Q may be viewed as a child's lifetime utility (as perceived by the parents); in this case, U becomes akin to a household-level social welfare function. We adhere to the first interpretation.

[4] We are assuming, of course, that the government can distinguish between child-specific commodities and adult-specific commodities.

T and B group-specific. In other words, the non-linear income tax schedules are approximated by linearising the budget constraint at the household equilibrium. The resulting *virtual* budget constraints will include household-specific tax parameters since in general the households will choose different combinations of pre-tax and post-tax income.

The time endowment is as always normalised to unity, so that the time constraint is,

$$N^h \lambda^h + l^h = 1, \tag{5.2}$$

where l is the labour supply. We substitute the time constraint into the budget constraint, so that we can write the latter as

$$q_x x^h + N^h \left[q_z z^h + \left(1 - \tau^h\right) w^h \lambda^h + B^h\right] = \left(1 - \tau^h\right) w^h + T^h, \tag{5.3}$$

with $\tau^h = \tau$, $T^h = T$ and $B^h = B$, $h = 1, 2$ when the tax system is linear. Note that the term in brackets on the l.h.s. of (5.3) is the marginal cost of a child and has therefore a natural interpretation as the "price of quantity". We will denote this price by

$$\pi^h = q_z z^h + \left(1 - \tau^h\right) w^h \lambda^h + B^h. \tag{5.4}$$

We will assume throughout the paper that $\pi^i > 0$; otherwise, our model would become one of children as assets. Note that π^h depends not only on the child benefit B^h, but also on the consumer price of the children-specific good, q_z and on the marginal rate of income tax, τ^h. The non-income taxes affect the actual expenditure on children, while the income tax affects the value of the time devoted to child attention (and therefore subtracted to the labour supply). Indeed, we can define the *effective* tax rate on children as

$$\theta^h = t_z z^h - \tau^h w^h \lambda^h + B^h; \tag{5.5}$$

if $\theta^h < 0$, then a child is a tax asset to his or her parents; if $\theta^h > 0$, it is a tax liability.

We can now characterise family behaviour in terms of first order conditions.[5] Maximising (5.1) subject to (5.3) by choice of C, z, h and N yields

$$U_c^h = \alpha^h q_x;\ U_Q^h Q_z^h = \alpha^h N^h q_z;\ U_Q^h Q_\lambda^h = \alpha^h N^h \left(1 - \tau^h\right) w^h;\ U_N^h = \alpha^h \pi^h \tag{5.6}$$

[5] In the literature on endogenous fertility, it is commonly assumed that N is a continuous variable, and that there is no uncertainty, and we follow this practice here. This is innocuous as long as one is not interested in the timing of births, but only in the number of them. It can be rationalized by taking the parents to be risk-neutral and viewing N as the expectation of a continuous approximation to the underlying discrete distribution of births. Note also that parental choices are, in principle, restricted also by a fertility "ceiling" (N cannot exceed some physiological maximum). However, when the fertility constraint is binding, the problem becomes one of exogenous fertility; hence, we will always assume that it is slack.

where α denotes the Lagrange multiplier on the budget constraint. Solving (5.6) plus the constraint, we derive the ordinary demand functions for x and z, the amount of time devoted to each child λ, and the fertility level N, as a function of the policy parameters. Substituting these back in the maximand gives us the indirect utility function $V(q_x, q_z, \tau, T, B; w)$. For future reference, note that the household's problem has a standard dual representation, in which expenditure is minimised subject to the attainment of a given utility level. The solution to this problem will give us the compensated demands $\widetilde{x}$ and $\widetilde{z}$, the compensated use of time $\widetilde{\lambda}$, and the compensated fertility level $\widetilde{N}$. Importantly, note that, due to the non-linearity of the budget constraints, the duality relations apply with a modification: the usual properties (Slutsky equation, symmetry, negativity of the own-price term, etc.) hold for x, $Z= zN$, $\Lambda = \lambda N$ and N and *not* for x, z, λ and N.[6] So, we have for instance that $\partial \widetilde{Z}/\partial B = \partial \widetilde{N}/\partial q$ by symmetry, and so on.

5.3 Establishing Benchmark Results

As we have always done so far, our main focus will be on second-best optimal tax structures when the government has a redistributive objective. It is illuminating, however, to establish first some benchmark results, which we do by briefly discussing first-best policy and efficiency-oriented second-best taxes. The characterisation of first best turns out to be useful for claryfing the role of the assumption that fertility is endogenous, while that of efficient second-best taxes helps us to understand that the rationale for child subsidies is entirely based on the presence of a redistributive objective.

5.3.1 First-Best Policy

As we have argued since Chap. 1, the assumption of endogenous fertility make sense on grounds of its empirical soundness. But a brief analysis of the first-best scenario will show that it avoids the risk of somehow introduce in the model a bias towards child subsidisation.

We argue first that, in first best, there is no reason to subsidise large families when fertility is endogenous. Suppose, in fact, that personalised lump-sum transfers are available. Then, of course, *all* distortionary taxation is redundant: we will have $\tau = t_x = t_z = B = 0$ at the optimum. Under the assumption that the government maximises a quasi-concave social welfare function with a purely redistributive objective, at the optimum high-wage families will be taxed and low-wage families

[6] To see this, simply note that the derivative of the expenditure function w.r.t. to q_z and w are $Z = zN$ (i.e. the total use of commodity z) and $\Lambda = \lambda N$, (i.e. the total amount of time devoted to children), respectively.

will be subsidised. How many children they have is not an issue: there is no reason to favour large families as such, because there is no sense in which large families have necessarily low utility.

However, assume now, for the sake of the argument, that fertility is exogenous. As we shall see, a rationale for subsidising large families will appear because of this. Write the budget constraint as

$$x^h + N^h \left(\left(z^h - \underline{z} \right) + \left(\lambda^h - \underline{\lambda} \right) w^h \right) = w^h + T^h - \left(\underline{z} + w^h \underline{\lambda} \right) N^h. \qquad (5.7)$$

The last term on the r.h.s represents the fixed costs of having children. There is no way in which these costs may be avoided by the parents, since they have no control on how large N is. Gross income is in fact $w - \left(\underline{z} + w\underline{h} \right) N$, not just w; and, clearly, gross income is decreasing in N. Then, first-best taxation will tend to favour large families, irrespective of their wage rate, because in this setting there is an obvious way in which having more children makes you poorer. Indeed if N^2 is much larger than N^1, it may well be the case that redistribution will be in favour of the high-wage families because they might be poorer in terms of "effective" gross income. Of course, this argument will carry over to a second-best setting: it will always be desirable to support households with many children, because of the higher costs they face. This makes clear that exogenous fertility models make a case for child subsidisation which is essentially based on the horizontal equity argument that parents should be compensated for the costs of procreation—give that such costs cannot be controlled by the parents in any way. As we argued, this is the basic reasoning behind the equivalence scales approach, which we reject.

5.3.2 *Second-Best Taxes When Only Efficiency Matters*

Let us ignore for a moment the differences in earning ability, and suppose that all households are identical (earn the same wage): this way, efficiency becomes the sole objective of the government. We can then manipulate our set of policy tools in order to shape the policy problem as a Ramsey-type problem. So, we eliminate T and normalise by imposing $\tau = 0$ (recall the discussion in Chap. 1); then, we choose optimally the indirect taxes and the tax on children by maximizing the indirect utility of a representative consumer under the constraint that $t_x x + t_z Z + BN = R$, where $R > 0$ is the revenue requirement. The standard result that all commodities (including children in our case) should be distorted uniformly holds (see e.g. Myles, 1995, Chap. 4).

Now, the Ramsey solution exhibits the well-known property that, if there is a positive revenue requirement, the (compensated) demand for all goods is discouraged. If cross-price effects are negligible, as it is widely assumed to be the case, this means that all tax rates are going to positive. Therefore, subsidisation of children is ruled out when the government only pursues an efficiency objective. Moreover, the effective tax rate on children θ—see above—will necessarily be positive; that is, children will always be a tax liability. The child-rearing technology determines the way in which the tax burden is allocated among the three tax bases. For example, suppose that the elasticity of substitution between z and λ is very low (approaching a Leontief technology): then the demand for z is basically insensitive to price changes, and therefore, to minimize distortions, most of the tax burden will be on z. Suppose instead that the elasticity of substitution between z and λ is very high (approaching a linear technology), so that the demand for z is extremely sensitive to price changes; in that case, the tax burden will be basically divided between x and N, and, if N is less own-price elastic than x, fertility will be heavily *taxed*. Finally, suppose that N is fixed, i.e. fertility is exogenous; then, the optimum would be reached by setting $B = R/N > 0$, because when a source of lump-sum taxation is available, no distortionary taxation is used. This allows us to establish that *no* case for subsidisation of children can be made when the government does *not* have a redistributive objective, no matter whether fertility is endogenous or exogenous.

5.4 Second-Best Taxes with a Redistributive Objective

Moving now to our main task, we take in turn the case in which the tax system is fully linear, and the one in which is mixed (non-linear income and children taxes plus linear indirect taxes). As we have already made clear, the redistributive impact of non-linear income tax schedules is much stronger; we therefore expect non income taxes to have a minor role as far as equity is concerned when the tax structure is mixed. This is indeed the case: commodity taxes supplementing a non-linear income tax are only helpful inasmuch as they help to relax the information-related constraints restricting the policy design. We will see that the same applies to the tax on children. On the contrary, non-income taxes play a substantial equitative role when the the tax structure is entirely linear. We shall see that the different relevance of non-income taxes in terms of redistributive impact is crucial in determining whether children should be subsidised or not.

5.4.1 Linear Tax System

In this case, we normalise the tax system by setting $\tau = 0$. Then, the government chooses t_x, t_z, B and T so as to maximise a Paretian, quasi-concave social welfare function subject to a revenue constraint:

$$\max \left\{ W\left(n^1 V^1, n^2 V^2\right) | t_x \sum_{h=1}^{2} n^h x^h + t_z \sum_{h=1}^{2} n^h Z^h + B \sum_{h=1}^{2} n^h N^h - T = R \right\}. \tag{5.8}$$

In order to characterise the tax rules, we define the net social marginal utility of income, inclusive of the effects of a marginal variation of income on revenue, as

$$\beta^h = \frac{W^h \alpha^h}{\mu} - t_x \sum_{h=1}^{2} n^h \frac{\partial x^h}{\partial T} - t_z \sum_{h=1}^{2} n^h \frac{\partial Z^h}{\partial T} - B \sum_{h=1}^{2} n^h \frac{\partial N^h}{\partial T}, \tag{5.9}$$

where $W^h = \partial W / \partial V^h$ is the welfare weight and μ is the Lagrange multiplier for the government's budget constraint (the social marginal value of revenue).

5.4.1.1 Optimal Tax Rules

From the first order condition for the optimal choice of T, we get, using (5.9),

$$\overline{b} = 1, \tag{5.10}$$

where the upper bar denotes an average value. That is, the marginal social value of raising one euro of revenue lump-sum, $\overline{b}$, should equal its marginal cost, 1. The optimal choice of t_x, t_z and B is instead governed by the many-person Ramsey tax rule, which, as we know from Chap. 1, is derived from the first order conditions in a standard way, using (5.10), the Slutsky equations and the symmetry of the Slutsky term:

$$D_k \equiv \frac{\sum_{h=1}^{2} n^h \left(t_x \frac{\partial \tilde{j}^h}{\partial t_x} + t_z \frac{\partial \tilde{j}^h}{\partial t_z} + B \frac{\partial \tilde{j}^h}{\partial G} \right)}{\sum_{h=1}^{2} n^h k^h} = -\left(1 - r_k\right), \quad j = x, Z, N, \tag{5.11}$$

where the "tilde" denotes a hicksian demand. The term on the l.h.s., denoted D_j, is the percentage change in the hicksian demand due to taxation (which we learned to call the "discouragement index"); finally

$$r_j = 1 + cov\left(\beta, j\right), \quad j = x, Z, N, \tag{5.12}$$

where cov denotes covariance, is the redistributive characteristic of good j, whose value exceeds (falls short of) unity if j is consumed prevalently by the households with low (high) β. So, the rules require that indirect taxes are designed in such a way that the consumption of commodity j is encouraged (discouraged) if it is mostly demanded by the high-β (low-b) families. As we know from Chap. 1, this implies that the tax system favours the less well-off, by encouraging the consumption of goods that they prevalently consume. It is interesting to check how this translates in terms of the tax treatment of children.

5.4.1.2 The Tax Treatment of Family Size

To interpret the tax rules in our setup, we need to place some structure on the model. We impose the following:

Assumption 1 $\beta^1 > \beta^2$;

Assumption 2 $\partial N/\partial w < 0$.

Assumption 1 is virtually always present in optimal taxation models: we have already used it repeatedly in the previous Chapters. It is actually rather mild. High-wagers have a larger pre-tax income than low-wagers (barring the case in which the labour supply curve is backward-bending): then, $W^2 \geq W^1$ under a quasi-concave social welfare function (i.e. if the government wants to redistribute towards the low-wagers), and $\alpha^2 > \alpha^1$ by the standard property of decreasing marginal utility of income: hence, Assumption 1 is established if the second, third and fourth term in the definition of β—see (5.9) above—are, as it is usually and plausibly assumed to be the case, second-order effects.

Assumption 2 is satisfied if the substitution effect of an increase in w prevails on the income effect, for then indeed the low-ability households would have more children than the high-ability ones. Intuitively, an increase in w implies a reduction in π; then, N increases if it behaves as a normal good relative to changes in π. Empirically, it is usually confirmed that high-earners tend to have fewer children than low-earners, so this may also be considered a mild restriction.

In order to arrive at a full characterization of the tax system, we need to know how adult and child consumption (x and Z) react to changes in the wage rate. To this end, we introduce an assumption which, as we saw in the previous Chapters, is widely used in optimal taxation theory[7] (in a simple consumption-leisure model it would be equivalent to the standard "single-crossing" assumption—see below), that is we postulate that

$$\partial x/\partial w > 0, \quad \partial Z/\partial w > 0. \tag{5.13}$$

The purpose of this assumption here is, however, solely that of making our arguments clearer by focusing on a specific case; perfectly analogous arguments can be developed under any assumption on the sign of $\partial x/\partial w$ and $\partial Z/\partial w$.

Once (5.13) is introduced, assumptions 1-2 are enough to establish a case for encouraging fertility as well as discouraging adult and child consumption: the tax system must be designed in such a way that the compensated fertility level increases,

[7] Recall that $Z = zN$; hence, in view of Assumption 2, we have that $\partial Z/\partial w > 0$ iff

$$\frac{\partial z}{\partial w}\frac{w}{z} > \left|\frac{\partial N}{\partial w}\frac{w}{N}\right|;$$

in turn, this requires that the child-rearing technology is characterised by a high elasticity of substitution between λ and z, so that an increase in w boosts the purchases of z. If we think of z as including marketed child-care services, this might indeed be a plausible situation.

and the compensated demands for adult- and child-specific goods decrease. To see this, simply note that the above assumptions imply that $r_x < 1$, $r_Z < 1$ and $r_N > 1$, because x and Z are prevalenty consumed by the low-β families (high-wagers) and N is larger in high-β families (low-wagers). Hence, it follows by (5.11) that:

$$D_x < 0; \quad D_Z < 0; \quad D_N > 0. \tag{5.14}$$

The intuition for this result is straightforward. Assumption 1 determines a perfectly negative correlation between wage (and income) levels and values of β: high-wagers (the "rich") have low social marginal utility of income, and low-wagers (the "poor") have high social marginal utility of income. The government is interested in redistributing towards the low-wage families, and, since the linear income tax is not very helpful in this respect, indirect taxation performs some redistribution by discouraging commodities that are prevalently consumed by the low-b, rich families (x and Z), and encouraging those that are prevalently consumed by the high-β, poor families (N).

5.4.1.3 The Policy Mix

The analysis so far has not, strictly speaking, given any indication on the sign of B (or, for that matter, of any other tax rate): this is, clearly, because the many-person Ramsey tax rules give the effects of taxation on quantities rather than on prices—as indeed all optimal tax rules. Indeed, we know that statements concerning the signs of the tax rates are not easy to make and should be treated with circumspection, since the tax rates are only defined up to a multiplicative constant (hence the normalisation). If a commodity faces a negative tax rate at the optimum, then this is to be interpreted as implying only that such commodity should be taxed less heavily that the untaxed good. In our case, if a child benefit emerges at the optimum, then the ensuing policy recommendation would be that children should receive a more favourable tax treatment than leisure.

With this proviso in mind, we can however attempt a characterisation of the policy mix. So far, we have established that family size should be *encouraged* and adult and child consumption should be *discouraged.* In principle, this is not the same as saying that the first should be *subsidised* ($B < 0$) and the other two should be *taxed* ($t_x > 0$, $t_z > 0$). However, it seems reasonable to conjecture that the optimal policy will encourage fertility by subsidising it and its complements, and taxing its substitutes; correspondingly, it will discourage adult and child consumption by taxing them and their complements, and subsidising their substitutes. This is indeed the most effective way to achieve the intended outcome. If the above conjecture is true, then it is easy to see that if, for example,

$$\frac{\partial \widetilde{x}}{\partial t_z} = \frac{\partial \widetilde{Z}}{\partial t_x} \leq 0; \quad \frac{\partial \widetilde{N}}{t_z} = \frac{\partial \widetilde{Z}}{\partial B} \geq 0; \quad \frac{\partial \widetilde{x}}{\partial B} = \frac{\partial \widetilde{N}}{\partial t_x} \geq 0, \tag{5.15}$$

a policy mix characterised by

$$B < 0, t_x > 0, t_z > 0 \tag{5.16}$$

satisfies the optimality conditions (5.11). Note that (5.15) imposes a restriction on the sign of the cross-substitution effects: adult and child consumption are regarded as complementary with each other and each of them is regarded as substitutable with the number of children. The reason why under (5.15) the policy mix in (5.16) may indeed be optimal is easily appreciated by noting that, for example, when x and N are substitutable with each other, a subsidy on N helps both to encourage it and to discourage x, and, similarly, a tax on x helps both to discourage it and to encourage N.[8]

Still, it is interesting to notice that, even if (5.16) actually prevails at the social optimum, it is not true that children are necessarily a tax asset to their parents: $\theta^h = t_z z^h + B$ (recall that $\tau = 0$) can have any sign.[9] The intuition behind this result is again linked to the need to perform redistribution largely using non-income taxes. Children have two dimensions, quantity and quality (approximated here by out-of-pocket expenditure, Z). Along the dimension of quantity they are a necessity (Assumption 2), but along the dimension of quality they might be a luxury—as implied by (5.13). Then, the government subsidises quantity and taxes quality; depending on which dimension prevails, the overall impact for the families may be positive (children become a tax asset) or negative (children become a tax liability).

5.4.2 Mixed Tax System

As we know, when the income tax is allowed to be non-linear, the policy design is restricted by the presence of information-related constraints. Since the government is choosing group-specific income tax parameters, it must guard itself against the risk that households belonging to one group might prefer the tax treatment intended for the members of the other group. This means that the tax rates have to be chosen under incentive-compatibility constraints such that the households self-select, i.e. reveal their true identity by choosing the tax treatment effectively intended for them. In principle, it is possible that high-wage households have to be prevented from masquerading as low-wage ones as well as the other way round. However, imposing the standard "single-crossing" condition that the indifference curves of the high-ability household are everywhere flatter than that of the low-ability ones in the (pre-

[8] Of course, whether (5.15) is an accurate description of actual preferences in any given society or not is ultimately an empirical matter. However, the variables involved—market transactions and the fertility level—are observable and therefore the validity of the assumption should be testable using normally available data. Moreover, the same policy mix can arise even under other assumptions on the signs of the cross-substitution effects.

[9] That, however, may change is we assume for example that $\partial Z/\partial w < 0$, for in that case the optimal policy mix would presumably include a subsidy for child consumption.

tax income, post-tax income)-space will result in only one constraint at the time to be binding; adding the assumption that the government wishes to redistribute from high- to low-ability households will guarantee that the only binding constraint is the one ruling out that high-ability households may choose the tax package intended for the other type. As we know, high-wage households misrepresenting their type are called "mimickers".

It may be useful to work out the mimicker's problem in some detail. As we know, since the government observes only pre-tax incomes (not hours worked or wage rates), the mimicker can adjust the labour supply in order to earn the same pre-tax income as the mimicked; as a consequence, it will have the same disposable income (the tax liability is the same), but it will work less than the true low-wage household (the mimicker's wage rate is higher). Moreover, and this is highly specific to the present setting, since also N^h is observable, the mimicker will also have to select the same number of children as the true low-ability households to avoid giving away its identity, $\widehat{N}^2 = N^1$.[10] That means that the mimicker has no choice of time allocation: using a "hat" to distinguish the variables pertaining to the mimicker, we have that it must work $\widehat{l}^2 = w^1 l^1 / w^2$ hours and devote $\widehat{\lambda}^2 = (1 - \widehat{l}^2)/\widehat{N}^2$ hours of attention to each children. The mimicker's problem will therefore be that of

$$\max_{C,z} \left\{ U\left(\widehat{x}^2, Q\left(\widehat{z}^2, \widehat{\lambda}^2\right), \widehat{N}^2\right) | t_x \widehat{x}^2 + \widehat{N}^2 \left[t_z \widehat{z}^2 + \left(1 - \tau^1\right) w^2 \widehat{\lambda}^2 + B^1 \right] = \left(1 - \tau^1\right) w^2 + T^1 \right\}, \tag{5.17}$$

taking the time allocation as given. This yields first order conditions

$$\widehat{U}_x^2 = \widehat{\alpha}^2 q_x; \quad \widehat{U}_Q^2 \widehat{Q}_z^2 = \widehat{\alpha}^2 q_z \widehat{N}^2. \tag{5.18}$$

Solving these together with the constraint will yield the optimal choices for C and z; substituting these back into the maximand will give us indirect utility, $\widehat{V}^2 = V(\tau^1, T^1, t_x, t_z, B^1; w^2)$.

It is interesting to notice that, relative to the standard model where only income is observable, the explicit consideration of children in the definition of the household's tax bill, imposes a further restriction on the mimicker's behaviour: as we just saw, since the mimicker must have the same income *and* the same number of children as the true low-wage household, then its time allocation is completely determined from the outside. We will study this point further in Chap. 6.

5.4.2.1 Optimal Tax Rules

Under a mixed tax system, it is convenient to normalise by setting one of the commodity tax rates to zero; we choose $t_z = 0$. Then, the government chooses t_x, G^h, τ^h

[10] Recall that N can be thought of as an expectation (footnote 5). Therefore, roughly speaking, the idea is that if the actual fertility level of the mimicker is realised with low probability by a true low-ability household, mimicking is not effective.

and T^h so as to maximise

$$\begin{aligned} \max\ & W\left(n^1V^1\left(\tau^1, T^1, t_x, B^1; w^2\right), n^2V^2\left(\tau^2, T^2, t_x, B^2; w^2\right)\right); \\ s.t.\ & V^2\left(t^2, T^2, t_x, G^2; w^1\right) \geq \widehat{V}^2\left(t^1, T^1, t_x, G^1; w^2\right), \{\sigma\} \\ & t_x \sum_{h=1}^{2} n^h x^h + \sum_{h=1}^{2} n^h B^h N^h + \sum_{h=1}^{2} n^h t^h w^h l^h - \sum_{h=1}^{2} n^h T^h = R, \{\mu\} \end{aligned}, \tag{5.19}$$

where the first constraint is the self-selection constraint and the second is the revenue constraint (the Lagrange multipliers are indicated in curly brackets). We do not provide the standard characterisation of the optimum income tax (see Chaps. 1 and 2), but simply give the *formulae* for the optimal indirect tax rate and the tax on children:

$$\sum_{h=1}^{2}\left(t_x n^h \frac{\partial \widetilde{x}^h}{\partial t_x} + B^h n^h \frac{\partial \widetilde{x}^h}{\partial B^h}\right) = \frac{\sigma\widehat{\alpha}^2}{\mu}(x^1 - \widehat{x}^2); \tag{5.20}$$

$$t_x n^h \frac{\partial \widetilde{N}^h}{\partial p} + B^h n^h \frac{\partial \widetilde{N}^h}{\partial G^h} = \frac{\sigma\widehat{\alpha}^2}{\mu}(N^1 - \widehat{N}^2) \equiv 0, \quad i = 1, 2. \tag{5.21}$$

To interpret these rules, note that on the l.h.s. we have a (variant of) the discouragement index, representing the marginal cost of using non-income taxes; at the optimum, this cost equals the marginal benefit, as given by the term on the r.h.s. This latter term is also well-known from our previous analysis and represents the relaxation of the self-selection constraint: its action is based on the fact that the mimicker normally has a different optimal bundle than the mimicked, despite having the same pre-tax income and the same disposable income. If, for example, $x^1 > \widehat{x}^2$, implying that the mimicker uses less of x than the true low-wage type, than it is optimal to encourage x (this follows because σ, μ and $\widehat{\alpha}^2$ are all positive); that is, the use of x is distorted in a way which is detrimental for the mimicker.

5.4.2.2 The Tax Treatment of Family Size and the Policy Mix

The above interpretation makes clear that, under a mixed tax system, the rationale for children subsidisation operating under a linear tax system disappears completely. From (5.21), we see that the gain in terms of self-selection of distorting fertility is zero: in other words, distorting fertility choices has no screening power, because the mimicker has the same number of children as the mimicked ($N^1 = \widehat{N}^2$). More specifically, the rule (5.21) says that B^h has to be set so as to totally offset the distortionary impact on N of the tax on x: net substitutability between x and N implies that B^h must have the same sign as t_x, whereas net complementarity implies that they should have opposite signs. So, for example, if x and N are net substitutes as in (5.15) and x is taxed, so must be N—the fact that the poor have more children does not justify, in this case, a favourable tax treatment for family size (Assumptions 1 and 2 play no role).

Still, this does not mean that children cannot be a tax asset. To see this in the context of a simple case, suppose that the utility function is separable in adult consumption on the one hand, and quality and quantity on the other; suppose further that the quality function is also separable in time and child consumption. For example, a utility function satisfying these restrictions would be

$$U^h = f\left(x^h\right) + \varphi\left(\varsigma\left(z^h\right) + \rho\left(\lambda^h\right), N\right). \tag{5.22}$$

Then, we have that all marketed commodities are separable from labour, that is the allocation of disposable income among its alternative uses does *not* depend on the time allocation. In that case, the mimicker and the genuine low-ability household, having the same disposable income and the same fertility level, also have the same consumption pattern, despite the fact that the mimicker has more non-working time. We have then re-created the conditions for the Atkinson and Stiglitz (1976) theorem to hold. Therefore, indirect taxation is redundant; indeed, $x^1 = \widehat{x}^2$ implies that $t_x = B^h = 0$, $h = 1, 2$, at the optimum. Moreover, we know that the standard characterisation of the marginal income tax rates holds: high-ability households are undistorted ($\tau^2 = 0$), while low-ability households are distorted for self-selection purposes ($\tau^1 > 0$)—see our previous Chapters. But then, it is easy to see that the effective tax rate on children for type-2 households is zero, while for type-1 households is negative ($\theta^1 = -\tau^1 w^1 \lambda^1 < 0$).

5.5 Concluding Remarks

In this Chapter, we endeavoured to shed more light on the issue whether benevolent governments should devise their optimal tax policies in such a way that children are subsidised. We did so under the assumption that parents act unitarily and that fertility is endogenous.

We found that when redistribution is accomplished mostly using non-income taxes, there is indeed a case for subsidising large families, although for unusual motivations. The main reason is indeed as follows: poor families tend to have more children, and it is therefore desirable to redistribute in favour of large households *not* because they are large, but because they are less well-off. Interestingly, this result does not depend on the *horizontal* equity-based arguments usually employed in the exogenous fertility literature; it is instead deeply rooted in a *vertical* equity requirement, i.e. the accomplishment of a redistributive objective on the government's part. Indeed, it is for this very fact that the desirability of encouraging family size vanishes when redistribution is accomplished mostly *via* the income tax; in that case, vertical equity is satisfied without distorting fertility.

In either case, however, the tax treatment of family size alone is not enough to determine whether a child should, on the whole, be a tax asset to his or her parents. Children affect parental well-being in different ways, depending on how many they are (their quantity) and how well they are treated (their quality); moreover, their cost includes an out-of-pocket expenditure as well as the shadow-value of the time not supplied to the labour market. Therefore, it is only by determining the signs of all the policy instruments that we can ascertain whether an extra-child increases or reduces the total tax bill of his or her parents.[11]

---

[11] There are several contributions to the literature on child benefits that illustrate how subsidising family size is far from a foregone conclusion: a particularly neat example is the paper by Blumkin et al. (2015), where the desirability of subsidising children, in a Beckerian quantity-quality model like ours and with an equity-oriented government, is shown to depend crucially on whether the benefits are means-tested or not.

Chapter 6
The Fiscal Treatment of Family Size: A Further Look

6.1 Introduction

In this Chapter we take a more detailed look at the fiscal treatment of family size under one of the tax systems reviewed in Chap. 5, namely the mixed tax system, and expand the household choice model by introducing bi-dimensional differences among household types. So, our concern is the design of a socially optimal system of direct and indirect taxes, constrained exclusively by the limits of the government's information, in a context of endogenous fertility—that is, in a context where the number and the well-being of the children are seen as the output of a special kind of home-production. The analysis, therefore, allows us to make a meaningful and complete comparison with the tax treatment of household production, which we studied in Chaps. 2 and 3 employing for the most part a mixed tax system and using a model with bi-dimensional differences. Furthermore, we can introduce a significant extension of the model by assuming that there are four, rather than two, household types. Our treatment is based mostly on Cigno (2001) and Balestrino et al. (2001, 2002).

As we briefly saw in the previous Chapter, in the standard case where households are differentiated by wage rates only and the government wishes to deploy a non-linear income tax in order to re-distribute in favour of low-wage households on the basis of observed incomes (wage rates and labour supplies are private information), mimicking can be discouraged more effectively if a household's total tax bill depends not only on income, but also on the number of children. Once we assume that parents have some control over the size of their progeny and we account for the fact that the number of children is observable by the government, we have to recognize that a high-wage household wanting to pass for a low-wage household would have to attain not only the same income level, but also the same number of children, as the latter. Clearly, that would impose a more stringent requirement on mimickers, and thus make mimicking more costly, than just having to obtain some target level of income.

A. Balestrino, *The Economics of Family Taxation*, Population Economics,
https://doi.org/10.1007/978-3-031-28170-9_6

One of the effects of allowing the government to use fertility information for its tax design would then be that of boosting the redistributive content of the income tax. The other interesting aspect, of course, would be to check the extent to which children have to be a tax asset or a tax liability for their parents. As we saw in the previous Chapter, this is a difficult question to settle in general: it is not however generally true that children should always be seen as tax assets, as it is instead both a common practice in many actual situations and a common theoretical result under exogenous fertility.

6.2 The Setup

In what follows, we apply once again the self-selection approach to the optimal choice of an extended set of policy instruments, that includes not only a non-linear income tax and linear commodity taxes, as usual, but also money transfers conditional on both income and number of children—which is still unusual in tax theory.

Household behaviour is described by a domestic production model with endogenous fertility. Households may differ in their ability to raise money, represented by the wage rate, w, but also in their ability to raise children, represented by a domestic productivity parameter, a. To begin with, we assume that there are only two possible values of both w and a, and only two possible household types. Clearly, w and a may be positively or negatively correlated (if a does not vary across households we might say that they are uncorrelated, but what it would really mean is that we are back to the case with one-dimensional differences): the characterization of the optimal tax system will not depend on the sign of the correlation, but, in trying to determine the signs of the various tax instruments, we shall consider the implications of positive or negative skill correlation. Later on, we will extend the model to include *four* types: this, at the expense of a few simplifications, will allow us to include a meaningful situation in which skills are actually uncorrelated.

Whatever the value of a, we refer to high-w households as type-2, and low-w households as type-1. The government knows individual preferences (assumed to be the same for every household) and the co-distribution of abilities (n^h households of each type), but cannot tell who is who. All the government can see is the income and the number of children each household has. Pre-tax prices are assumed to be invariant with respect to government policy, and normalized to unity. Since market transactions are anonymous, however, the government cannot tell whether a purchaser is of type 1 or of type 2. This implies that commodity taxation must be *linear*. On the other hand, since fertility is observable, taxes on the number of children may be *non-linear*.

The government sets the rate of tax on child-specific commodities, t_z (the rate of tax on adult-specific commodities is normalized to zero), and a household tax schedule relating after-tax income to pre-tax income and number of children. Given that there are only two household types, that is the same as offering households a menu $\left(t_z, B^h, b^h, y^h\right)$, $h = 1, 2$, where B^h, b^h and y^h are, respectively, the tax (subsidy) rate on number of children, and household income before and after income tax, intended for household type h.[1] The income tax for that type of household is $T(y^h) = y^h - b^h$. Recalling that, due to the normalisation, all tax rates are to be interpreted in relative terms, we can say that a negative (positive) value of t_z means that child-specific commodities are taxed less (more) than adult-specific commodities. A negative (positive) value of B^h means that type-h households receive a subsidy (pay a tax) on the number of children they have. Given these taxes and subsidies, households choose their consumption/reproduction plans, which may involve concealing their true characteristics in order to benefit from the more favourable tax treatment intended for the other household type. In choosing the policy mix, the government takes these behavioural responses into account.

6.2.1 Households

Just as in Chap. 5, household preferences are described by the utility function

$$U^h = U(x^h, Q^h, N^h), \tag{6.1}$$

where x is adult consumption, Q an index of the children's quality of life ("quality" for short), and N the number ("quantity") of children. Clearly, Q will depend on the quantity of child-specific commodities, z, and parental time ("attention"), λ, provided to each child, and, in this case, also on the domestic ability parameter a:

$$Q^h = Q(z^h, \lambda^h; a^h). \tag{6.2}$$

Denoting by $(\underline{z}, \underline{\lambda})$ the minimum levels of z and h necessary to bring a child into the world, and to keep him or her alive, we can set the scale of Q so that $Q\left(\underline{z}, \underline{\lambda}; a\right) = 0$. The function $Q(\cdot; k)$ will be taken to be homogeneous of degree one in $\left(z - \underline{z}, h - \underline{h}\right)$.

The household budget constraint is

$$x^h + (1 + t_z)Z^h + B^h N = b, \tag{6.3}$$

where $Z \equiv Nz$ is the household's total demand for child-specific commodities. Normalizing the time endowment (of adult household members) to unity, we can write the time-budget constraint as

$$\Lambda^h + l^h = 1, \tag{6.4}$$

[1] An alternative and equivalent way of representing the policy would be to say that the government offers households a menu $\left(t_z, N^h, b^h, y^h\right)$, $h = 1, 2$. This way, we would treat the two observable variables, income and number of children, symmetrically. However, from an analytical standpoint, it would be rather complicated to handle a *linear* tax on child-specific commodities and a *non-linear* tax on number of children at the same time, both affecting the decision to have children. It is much easier to employ an income-contingent, piece-wise linear tax (subsidy) on the number of children; the results are of course identical.

where $\Lambda \equiv N\lambda$ is the total amount of time allocated to the care of children, and l the labour supply.

Adult household members choose expenditures and time allocation and, within the natural bounds on fertility, they also choose how many children to have. We have already noticed in similar situations that the kind of setup we are using here, in which comparative advantages come into play, presents an asymmetry when it come to specialisation (Chap. 2). Indeed, if labour were the household's only source of finance, and the government were absent ($b = y = wl$), the households could completely specialise in market works, if they wished, but could not realise a complete specialisation in domestic activities: the budget constraint would prevent that, because the households would have to sell some of their time to the labour market in order to pay for Z. As we already know, this asymmetry has important policy implications.

We can now proceed along well-trodden paths. Since $l = y/w$, choosing y is the same as choosing l. Since government policy effectively restricts household choice to a finite number of alternatives (actually two, one intended for type 1, the other intended for type 2), we can describe household choice as a two-step decision procedure. First, the household finds the (x, N, z, λ) that maximizes household utility for any given (t_z, B, b, y). Second, it selects, from the menu offered by the government, the (t_z, B, b, y) with the higher maximized utility (i.e., effectively, declares to be either type 1, or type 2).

A household choosing the policy constellation that was intended for its own type maximizes (6.1), subject to (6.2)–(6.4). The solution satisfies

$$U_x^h = \alpha^h; \quad U_Q^h Q_z^h = \alpha^h N^h (1 + t_z); \\ U_N^h = \alpha^h \left[(1 + t_z) z^h + B^h \right] + \kappa^h \lambda^h; \quad U_Q^h Q_\lambda^h = \kappa^h N^h, \tag{6.5}$$

where α and κ are the marginal utilities of, respectively, income and time, and subscripts denote partial differentiation. Solving these first-order conditions together with the constraints gives us the household demands for (x, N, z, λ) as functions of the policy instruments. Substituting back into the utility function, gives us the indirect utility function, $V(t_z, B, b, y; w, a)$.

The marginal utilities of income before and after income tax are, respectively, $V_y = -\kappa/w$ and $V_b = \alpha$. The negative sign of the first expression is due to the fact that a rise in y, holding w constant, implies a rise in labour supply. Using (6.5), and $T(y) \equiv y - b$, we find

$$T'(y^h) = 1 - \frac{\kappa^h}{\alpha^h w^h}. \tag{6.6}$$

The right-hand-side of the first-order condition for N in (6.5) represents the marginal cost of N. Denoting by $\Delta \equiv t_z z + B$ the effective tax on money spent for each child, and using (6.6), we may re-write this marginal cost as

$$\pi^h \equiv z^h + \Delta + \left[w^h - T'(y^h) \right] \lambda^h, \tag{6.7}$$

This shows that the cost of an extra child is the sum of an actual expenditure ($z + \Delta$), and an opportunity-cost $\left[w - T'(y)\right]\lambda$. An additional child of zero "quality" (i.e., a child who receiced from his parents only the bare necessities of life) costs

$$\underline{\pi} \equiv t(1 + t_z)\underline{z} + B^h + \left[w^h - T'(y^h)\right]\underline{\lambda}. \tag{6.8}$$

We may think of this as the fixed cost of a child.

Notice that the marginal cost of N, π, is affected by *all* the policy instruments, while the marginal cost of Q,

$$\left(\pi^h - \underline{\pi}\right) N^h = \left(t_z\left(z^h - \underline{z}\right) + \left[w^h - T'(y^h)\left(\lambda^h - \underline{\lambda}\right)\right) N \tag{6.9}$$

is independent of B. Therefore, a tax (subsidy) on the number of children distorts marginal incentives in favour of child quality (quantity).[2]

For future reference, we recall that, as far as the duality properties of the household optimization problem are concerned, the standard results cannot be applied directly, due to the non-linearity of the budget constraint (see Chap. 5). It is possible to show, however, that the Slutsky relations apply to x , $Z = zN$, $\Lambda = \lambda N$, N and *not* to x, z, h and N.

6.2.2 Mimickers

If different household types receive different tax treatment, it may be in the interest of a type-h household to pretend to be type-k ($h, k = 1, 2$). If that is the case, we call this household an "hk-mimicker".[3] As we know, in conventional optimal income taxation models, it is customary to impose the agent monotonicity condition that $-V_y/V_b$ is decreasing in the wage rate. When households are differentiated by earning ability only, this implies that the indifference curves in the (b, y)-plane are everywhere flatter for high-wage than for low-wage households ("single-crossing"). Normally, one would combine agent monotonicity with the assumption that the policy maker's preferences exhibit inequality aversion (i.e. the social welfare function is quasi-concave and redistribution is in favour of low-wage households), so as to restrict mimicking behaviour to the high-wagers: since the tax system favours the low-wage households, they will not be interested in mimicking a high-wage one. We however employ a more general set-up with households differing by more than just wage rates, and since we do not *a priori* know whether high-wagers or low-wagers would be favoured by the tax system, it is possible that either household type could have an interest in concealing its true identity.

---

2 This point was first noted in Cigno (1986).

3 Since we are now considering two possible mimickers, the "hat" is not enough to identify the mimicker.

As we know, a h-type household wanting to mis-represent its type will set the choice variables that the government can observe equal to those of type-k households. Suppose for a moment that the government can only observe incomes, which is the standard setup: in that case, the mimicker could become indistinguishable from the mimicked simply by adjusting its labour supply. In our setup, however, the government can also observe the number of children: therefore, to avoid giving away its true identity, the mimicket must also choose to have the same number of children as the mimicked. Summing up, an hk-mimicker will have the same gross income, y^k, as well as the same fertility, N^k, as the mimicked. As we know from Chap. 5, what this means is that a mimicker has no choice of time allocation: it must devote (y^k/w^h) hours to the labour market, and $[(w^h - y^k)/w^k]$ hours to looking after children.[4]

The mimicker's optimization,

$$\begin{array}{ll} \max_{x,z} & U^{hk} = U\left[x^{hk}, Q^{hk}\left(z^{hk}, \frac{(w^h - Y^k)}{w^h N^k}\right), N^k\right] \\ \text{s.t.} & x^{hk} + \left[(1+t_z)z^{hk} + B^k\right]N^k = b^k, \end{array} \tag{6.10}$$

has first-order conditions

$$U_x^{hk} = \alpha^{hk}; \quad U_Q^{hk} Q_z^{hk} = \alpha^{hk} N^k (1 + t_z). \tag{6.11}$$

The indirect utility function that emerges from this optimization is $V^{hk} = V(t_z, B^k, b^k, y^k; w^h, a^h)$, $h \neq k$.

6.3 Optimal Taxation

As we have done several times before, we assume that the government's aim is to maximize a Paretian, quasi-concave social welfare function, W, in which the indirect utilities of the two household types appear as arguments. The optimal choice of policy instruments faces two types of constraints: first, the government budget constraint, and, second, the self-selection constraints that neither household type must be better-off mimicking than being truthful. To keep things simple, we take it that the government has no revenue requirement (in other words, taxation is purely re-distributive); so, the optimal policy problem is to choose $(t_z, B^1, B^2, b^1, b^2, y^1, y^2)$ so as to

---

[4] This is of course somewhat extreme and comes from the fact that, in our mode, there are no other way of using time than for making money or raising children, both being activities that have an observable output. If we were to allow for more alternatives (*e.g.* leisure), the mimicker would then have some choice of time allocation and mimicking would be more difficult to deter. However, the present model is not too restrictive, both because children are extremely time-intensive (so that the time for leisure would not be much anyway) and because, if leisure activities are costly to monitor (or, in general, if the alternative use of non-labour time has no observable output, the policy results do not change, as shown in Cigno (2001).

$$\begin{array}{llr}
\max & W\left[V\left(t_z, B^1, y^1, b^1; w^1, a^1\right), V\left(t_z, B^2, y^2, b^2; w^2, a^2\right)\right] & \\
\text{s.t.} & V\left(t_z, B^1, y^1, b^1; w^1, a^1\right) \geq V\left(t_z, B^2, y^2, b^2; w^1, a^1\right), & \left[\sigma^{12}\right] \\
& V\left(t_z, B^2, y^2, b^2; w^2, a^2\right) \geq V\left(t_z, B^1, y^1, b^1; w^2, a^2\right), & \left[\sigma^{21}\right] \\
& \sum_h n^h\left(t_z Z^h + B^h N^h + Y^h - B^h\right) = 0, & [\mu]
\end{array} \tag{6.12}$$

where the symbols in square brackets are the Lagrange-multipliers.

Denoting by $W_h \equiv \partial W/\partial V^h > 0$ the welfare weight of a type-i household, we can write the first-order conditions for the policy optimisation as

$$\left(W_h + \sigma^{hk}\right) V_y^h - \sigma^{kh} V_y^{kh} + \mu\left[1 + t_z Z_y^h + B^h N_y^h\right] = 0, \quad h, k = 1, 2, h \neq k; \tag{6.13}$$

$$\left(W_h + \sigma^{hk}\right) V_b^i - \sigma^{kh} V_b^{kh} + \mu - 1 + t_z Z_b^h + B^h N_b^h] = 0, \quad h, k = 1, 2, h \neq k; \tag{6.14}$$

$$\left(W_h + \sigma^{hk}\right) V_B^h - \sigma^{kh} V_B^{kh} + \mu\left[t_z Z_B^h + N^h + B^h N_B^h\right] = 0, \quad h, k = 1, 2, h \neq k; \tag{6.15}$$

$$\sum_h\left(W_i + \sigma^{hh}\right) V_{t_z}^h + \sum_h \sigma^{ih} V_{t_z}^{kh} + \mu \sum_h n^h\left[Z^h + s Z_{t_z}^h + t^h N_{t_z}^h\right] = 0. \tag{6.16}$$

As a benchmark case, let us focus first on a situation in which neither self-selection constraint is binding (i.e., at the optimum, both types of households reveal their true characteristics). In that case, we have a first best outcome, as the government can carry out the desired re-distribution using lump-sum transfers. If either of the self-selection constraints is binding, however, we move into second best territory: the government needs to introduce distortions, using taxes that alter marginal incentives, so as to induce the households to reveal their true type. At this stage, we cannot say which of the self-selection constraints will be binding (actually, neither of them might, in principle)[5]: this depends on the direction of redistribution as well as on the optimal choice of policy instruments. The point, of course, is that in the present setup the high-wage household is not necessarily better-off. Thus, if redistribution is from high to low-wage households, then $\sigma^{21} > 0$ and $\sigma^{12} = 0$; otherwise, $\sigma^{12} > 0$ and $\sigma^{21} = 0$.

6.3.1 The Direction of Re-distribution

We can rely now on the findings illustrated in Chap. 2. The direction of re-distribution is important, not only for its own sake, but also for self-selection purposes. If households were differentiated by their wage rate, i.e. by their labour market ability, only, as it is commonly done in optimal taxation models, redistribution would be driven by

[5] Actually, both self-selection constraints might be binding at the same time. This would be, however, a technical curiosity without much economic interest. There are various technical assumptions that can be used to rule it out. Sufficient conditions are for example: (i) the marginal utility of income is non-decreasing in the wage-rate, (ii) the marginal utility of time is non-increasing in the wage rate, (iii) both are invariant with respect to the domestic ability parameter. We assume these to be satisfied.

"equity" reasons, and would therefore go from high to low-w households (who, in that context, surely have lower *laissez-faire* utility). As we argued in Chap. 2, however, if households are differentiated also by their ability in the domestic production of non-tradable goods (which, in this case, are N and Q, i.e. the number of children and their quality of life), then, there can be an "efficiency", as well as an "equity", motive for re-distribution.

The upshot is that the direction of redistribution becomes less obvious to anticipate. To see this, consider for example the following argument. We know that, in order to pursue allocative efficiency gains, households should specialize according to their comparative advantage. So, if $a^h/w^h > a^k/w^k$, then household h should specialise in domestic activities, that is raising its children, while household k should specialise in market activities, that is earning an income. As we already know from our analysis in Chap. 2, however, the budget constraint may prevent type-h households from specializing completely in domestic activities. Since the same restriction does not apply in the opposite direction (nothing would stop type-k households from specializing completely in market activities, if they so wished), re-distributing towards households that are comparatively better at raising children could then raise welfare, quite independently of equity considerations, simply because it would allow the beneficiaries to pursue their comparative advantage more fully.

Consider, first, the case of negative correlation between domestic and market skills, that is $a^1 > a^2$, and $a^1/w^1 > a^2/w^2$. Interestingly, in this setting, low-w households have a comparative advantage in raising children, but do not necessarily have lower *laissez-faire* utility than high-w households, because a^1 may be sufficiently larger than a^2 to make type-1 households better-off than type-2 in the absence of policy. Only when a^1 is not large enough, then redistribution is unambiguously in favour of the low-wagers, because then equity and efficiency considerations pull in the same direction: type-1 agents are both abler at raising children and poorer than type-2 agents. Then, we will have $\sigma^{12} = 0$ and $\sigma^{21} > 0$.

However, if skills are negatively correlated and a^1 is so large that type-1 households are better-off, in utility terms, at the *laissez-faire* equilibrium, than type-2 households, then we cannot establish *a priori* the direction of redistribution: equity suggests that the optimal tax system favour the high-wagers, but efficiency (the pursuit of comparative advantages) suggests the opposite. Ultimately, the outcome depends on the extent to which the policy maker is inequality-adverse, that is how convex the social indifference curves are. Equity will certainly prevail if the social welfare function is Rawlsian, because then after-tax utilities have to be equal. But, to take to opposite example, if the social welfare function is utilitarian, the efficiency motive will presumably prevail: a Benthamite social planner is interested in maximising the sum of the utilities, and only pursues equity if this increases such a sum. If the social planner is Benthamite, then, re-distribution would possibly be in favour of low-w households ($\sigma^{12} = 0$, $\sigma^{21} > 0$) even though they are better-off to begin with: taking from the worse-off and giving to the better-off is justified if it increases the sum of utilities, i.e. if those negatively affected experience a reduction in utility which is more than compensated by the increase in utility for those who are positively affected. In the intermediate case of a generic strictly quasi-concave social welfare function, re-distribution *might* be in favour of high-w households and, if inequality aversion is sufficiently large, we could then have $\sigma^{12} > 0$ and $\sigma^{21} = 0$.

Next, consider the case in which $a^1 < a^2$, that is skills are *positively* correlated. The situation is now reversed relative to the case of negative correlation. Type-1 housholds have both lower wagers and lower domestic ability than type-2 households, and therefore have lower *laissez-faire* utility; however, we do not know whether they have a comparative advantage in raising children or not. If $a^1/w^1 > a^2/w^2$, then we can be certain that re-distribution is in favour of low-w households, because both equity and efficiency considerations require it ($\sigma^{12} = 0$, $\sigma^{21} > 0$). However, if $a^1/w^1 < a^2/w^2$, equity still suggest that low-wagers are favoured by the tax system, while efficiency pulls in the opposite direction. As a result, re-distribution is likely to be be in favour of low-wage households ($\sigma^{12} = 0$, $\sigma^{21} > 0$) starting from the Rawlsian case and as long as if social preferences are sufficiently inequality-adverse, but might be in favour of high-wage households ($\sigma^{12} > 0$, $\sigma^{21} = 0$) when social preferences approach the utilitarian case.

As already mentioned, with only two household types, the case of no skill correlation is really nothing but the case of one-dimensional differentiation. Indeed, since we take $w^1 < w^2$ to be always satisfied, the absence of correlation means trivially $a^1 = a^2$. Households then differ for their wage rate only as in the standard optimal taxation model - we treated this case in Chap. 5.

6.3.2 Taxes on Income

Denoting by $\Theta^h\left(y^h, N^h\right) \equiv \left(t_z Z^h + B^h N^h + y^h - b^h\right)$ the total tax bill of a type-h household, and using (6.6), we find the marginal effective rate of income tax,

$$\Theta^i_Y = T'\left(y^h\right) + t_z Z_y + B^h N_y \equiv 1 + \frac{V_y}{V_b} + t_z Z_y + B^h N_y. \qquad (6.17)$$

Adapting the procedure in Edwards et al. (1994) that we already used in Chap. 1 and elsewhere, we find the following expressions for the optimal marginal income tax rates:

$$T'\left(y^1\right) = \frac{\sigma^{21} V_b^{21}}{\mu}\left(\frac{V_y^{21}}{V_b^{21}} - \frac{V_y^1}{V_b^1}\right) - n^1\left[t_z \widetilde{Z}_y^1 + B^1 \tilde{N}_y^1\right], \qquad (6.18)$$

$$T'\left(y^2\right) = \frac{\sigma^{12} V_b^{12}}{\mu}\left(\frac{V_y^{12}}{V_b^{12}} - \frac{V_y^2}{V_b^2}\right) - n^2\left[t_z \tilde{Z}_y^2 + B^1 \tilde{N}_y^2\right], \qquad (6.19)$$

where the "tilde" denotes a compensated demand. To interpret these rules, let us for a moment imagine a situation which brings us back at the standard analysis of the income tax, in which there are no indirect taxes and the direction of redistribution is from high- to low-wagers. Then, we will have no taxes on children or commodities, meaning that both second r.h.s. terms in the two expressions are identically zero. Also, we will have that $\sigma^{21} > 0$ and $\sigma^{12} = 0$, i.e., at the optimum, type-2 households are interested in mimicking type-1 households, but the latter are not interested in mimicking the former. Assuming that the standard single-crossing condition, whereby at the optimal (b^1, y^1), the indifference curve of a low-wage household is steeper than that of a high-wage mimicker, holds, then the presence of a positive marginal income tax rate on type-1 households would discourage mimicking (at the cost, obviously, of distorting the low-wagers' choices). On the other hand, since type-1 households have no incentive to mimic the high-wagers, a positive marginal rate of income tax on the latter would be pointless, as it would distort their decisions without generating any advantage. In this particular case, then, (6.18)–(6.19) would reduce to $T'(y^1) > 0$ and $T'(y^2) = 0$, which is basically the standard no-distortion-at-the-top property of conventional optimal income taxation models. In general, however, σ^{12} could be positive, therefore the marginal rate of income tax on high earners might differ from zero.

Moreover, if we re-introduce indirect taxes, the picture changes again - this is also something that we already explored in Chap. 1 and elsewhere. In this specific setting, indirect taxation takes the form of taxes (subsidies) on child-specific commodities or the number of children. If they are present, there is a revenue effect represented by the terms in square brackets in (6.18)–(6.19). Suppose, for example, that $[t_z \widehat{Z}^2_y + B^1 \widehat{N}^2_y] < 0$. In this case, the revenue from taxing commodities and number of children is decreasing in the labour supply of type-2 households. This yields an additional reason, independent of self-selection considerations, for distortionary income taxation, because in that case, even if nobody were interested in mimicking the high earners $(\sigma^{12} = 0)$, it would be required at the optimum to have a positive marginal rate of income tax on them so as to raise tax revenue.

We can then conclude that the standard no-distortion-at-the-top proposition does not hold in the present model for two independent reasons. First, because either self-selection constraint could be binding, even with a quasi-concave social welfare function. Second, because there may be a revenue effect. The first departure from the standard result is due to the structure of the present model, in particular to the bi-dimensional differentiation of households. The second, not specific to our model, arises whenever there are other forms of taxation alongside an income tax, and has indeed been already explained in Chap. 1, where we illustrated how in that case the no-distortion-at-the-top result holds for the marginal *effective* tax rate.

6.3.3 Taxes on Commodities, and Taxes on Number of Children

We can now consider (6.15) and (6.16). Following the usual steps and noting that $N^{kh} = N^h$, we find

$$t_z \overset{\sim h}{N}_{t_z} + B^h \overset{\sim h}{N}_B = 0, \quad h = 1, 2, \tag{6.20}$$

and

$$\sum_h n^h \left(t_z \overset{\sim h}{Z}_t + B^h \overset{\sim h}{Z}_B \right) = N^1 \frac{\sigma^{21} V_b^{21}}{\mu} (z^1 - z^{21}) + N^2 \frac{\sigma^{12} V_b^{12}}{\mu} (z^2 - z^{12}). \tag{6.21}$$

The l.h.s. of (6.29) is yet another instance of the discouragement index and measures the cost of distorting the demand for child-specific commodities through t_z and B^h as the compensated effect on Z . If the effect is negative (positive) we say that the demand for child-specific commodities is "discouraged" ("encouraged"). The r.h.s. represents the corresponding gain. To see the intuition behind the rule, suppose, for instance, that $\sigma^{21} > 0, \sigma^{12} = 0$ and $z^1 < z^{21}$ (i.e., that true type-1 households spend less, for each of their children, than 21-mimickers). Since V_b^{21} and μ are positive, it is clear that, in this case, distorting prices in favour of adult-specific commodities would harm mimickers more than genuine low-wage households. Therefore, the relevant self-selection constraint can be relaxed by discouraging the purchase of child-specific commodities. Analogous considerations apply to the other possible cases.

As for (6.30), its l.h.s. measures the cost of distorting fertility decisions through t_z and B, while its r.h.s. measures the corresponding gain, which is however zero. This occurs because fertility is observable by the government: the mimicking household must therefore have the same number of children as the mimicked one, otherwise it would give itself away. As a consequence, distorting fertility choices has no "screening power": in other words, indirect taxes must *not* distort fertility decisions.

The fact that there is no point in using t_z and B^h to distort fertility decisions because such a fiscal maneuver cannot be used to discourage mimicking does not imply, however, that $B^h = 0$. As long as (6.29) provides a second-best rationale for taxing or subsidizing child-specific commodities, the policy prescription is in fact to set B^h so that it totally offsets the distortionary effect of t_z on the number of children (not on the child-specific commodities). More specifically, (6.30) tells us that t_z and B^h must have *opposite signs* if Z and N are Hicksian *complements*, the *same sign* if Z and N are Hicksian *substitutes*. Only when $t_z = 0$, then $B^h = 0$ at the optimum. In turn, that can only happen when the demand for Z is independent of both a and w, for then mimickers would buy the same amount of the child-specific commodities as the mimicked, and the r.h.s. of (6.29) would consequently be zero.

Furthermore, recall that t_z and B^h are not the only policy instruments affecting the cost of raising children. Hence, even if they were both zero, (6.30) would still not imply that fertility should be undistorted at a second-best optimum. To see this, consider (6.7). It is immediate to realise that, even if $t_z = B^h = 0$, the post-tax price of children would still differ from the pre-tax price, as long as $T'(y) \neq 0$ (by taxing income at the margin, the government reduces the opportunity-cost of child-bearing). Moreover, even if $T'(y) = 0$, fertility decisions would still be distorted as long as child-specific commodities or the number of children are taxed or subsidized, since

$t_z z^h + B^h$ is different from zero if t_z and B^h have the same sign, and needs not be zero even if they have opposite signs (in general, $|t_z z^h| \neq |B^h|$). To sum up, the observability of children makes it pointless to distort fertility decisions for the sake of discouraging mimicking, but other grounds for distortion remain valid: for example, for distributional reasons, or in order to counter the effects of other distortions.

The *effective* marginal tax rate on children is found by differentiating the total tax bill of a type-i household with respect to N^i,

$$\Theta_N^h = \Delta^h - T'(y^h) w^h \lambda^h = \vartheta^h + \frac{\varkappa^h \lambda^h}{\alpha^h} - w^h \lambda^h, \tag{6.22}$$

where $\Delta^h \equiv t_z z^h + B^h$ and the second equation sign follows from (6.6). The sign of Θ_N^h tells us whether a child should be a tax asset or a tax liability for that household type. In first best, where there is no distortionary taxation, children are clearly tax neutral for every type of household (this was established by Nerlove et al. 1987). In second best, it depends on the number of characteristics by which households are differentiated, and on the number of tax instruments available. If households are differentiated by the wage rate only, as in the standard optimal taxation model, and there is only an income tax, children must be tax neutral for high earners (the potential mimickers), but a tax asset for low-wage households. With taxes or subsidies on child-specific commodities or number of children, however, anything is possible, because Δ^h can have any sign. The same is true if households are differentiated by more than one characteristic, because then both Δ^h and $T'(y^h)$ can have any sign.

6.4 Redistributive Policy with Four Household Types

We maintain now the assumption that the government can use non-linear taxes on income and number of children, as well as linear taxes on commodities, but we extend the model by allowing for *four* household types. As we already noticed, with two types and two characteristics, the latter have necessarily to be correlated, either positively or negatively - the case of no-correlation is basically the one in which the domestic ability parameter does not vary across household, so that we fall back into the one-dimensional case. With four types, by contrast, it is also possible to have a meaningful no correlation scenario. We thus assume that there are two possible values of w and a, $w^1 < w^2$ and $a^L < a^H$, and four possible household types, $h = 1L, 1H, 2L, 2H$. As usual, there are n^h households of each type and the total population is normalised to unity.

As highlighted in Cremer et al. (2000), this introduces additional complexities regarding the direction of redistribution and the pattern of binding self-selection constraints. In order to make things simpler, we take it that the government's aim is to maximize a Rawlsian social welfare function. This will result in equal after-policy utility levels for all household types. To properly identify the government's objective function, we first have to establish which household type would have the lowest utility level in a *laissez-faire* situation. Under the natural assumption that utility is increasing in both w and a, the household type that would fare worse without policy intervention is clearly $1L$. The government will therefore maximize the utility of type-$1L$ households, subject to the budget constraint, as well as to the self-selection constraints that households must not be better-off mimicking, than behaving according to type. Assuming, for simplicity, that the government has no revenue requirement (and indicating the Lagrange-multipliers in square brackets), the problem is to choose $\left(t_z, B^h, b^h, y^h\right)$ so as to

$$\begin{aligned} &\max\ V^{1L} \\ &\text{s.t.}\ \ V^{1L} \geq V^{1L,k}, \quad k = 1H, 2L, 2H \qquad \left[\sigma^{1L,k}\right] \\ &\qquad V^{1H} \geq V^{1H,k}, \quad k = 1L, 2L, 2H \qquad \left[\sigma^{1H,k}\right] \\ &\qquad V^{2L} \geq V^{2L,k}, \quad k = 1L, 1H, 2H \qquad \left[\sigma^{2L,k}\right] \\ &\qquad V^{2H} \geq V^{2H,k}, \quad k = 1L, 1H, 2L \qquad \left[\sigma^{2H,k}\right] \\ &\qquad \textstyle\sum_h n^h \left(t_z Z^h + B^h N^h + y^h - b^h\right) = 0. \ [\mu] \end{aligned} \tag{6.23}$$

In order to characterise the optimal policy, we have to identify the pattern of binding self-selection constraints. If none of them is binding (i.e., households reveal their true characteristics), the government can carry out the desired redistribution by lump-sum transfers, and the solution is a first best. We did not study this case in the two-type scenario, but it can be shown to be a possibility (see Cigno et al., 2002). In the present scenario, however, this could occur only if the *laissez-faire* outcome happened to be very close to the Ralwsian optimum, which in turn could be true only if differences across households were small. In general, therefore, *some* self-selection constraints will be binding.

For simplicity, we shall assume that there is no "bunching".[6] Then, each household will want to mimic those households whose tax treatment is more favourable than its own. Since the government is egalitarian in the extreme, and will thus want to take from the better-off in order to give to the worse-off in all conceivable situations, the direction of redistribution depends on the ranking of utility levels in the *laissez-faire* equilibrium. We already know that $1L$-households are going to be the ones with the lowest welfare level when utility is increasing in both distinguishing characteristics. By the same token, $2H$-households will have the highest welfare level. The relative position of the other two types is ambiguous, but the more interesting case is arguably the one in which in which $1H$-households fare better than $2L$-households, for then the utility ranking does not reflect the ranking in terms of earning ability.[7] We therefore proceed on the basis of

- **Assumption 1**. At the laissez-faire equilibrium, households' utilities are ranked as follows:

[6] If all households with abilities falling in a given interval earn the same pre-tax income, they are said to be "bunched" at a single income level.

[7] The other case is entirely symmetric. We leave it to the reader to work out the details.

$$U^{2H} > U^{1H} > U^{2L} > U^{1L}. \tag{6.24}$$

Given Assumption 1 is easy to see that, with Ralwsian social preferences and no bunching,

1. there will be no $(1L, k)$-mimickers, that is $\sigma^{1L,k} = 0$, all k;
2. $2L$-households will mimic only $1L$-households, that is $\sigma^{2L,k} = 0$, $k = 1H, 2H$ and $\sigma^{2L,1L} > 0$;
3. $1H$-households would mimic $1L$- and $2L$-households, but not $2H$-households, that is $\sigma^{1H,2H} = 0$ and $\sigma^{1H,k} > 0$, $k = 1L$ or $k = 2L$
4. $2H$-household would mimic all other three types, that is $\sigma^{2H,k} > 0$, for one k

6.4.1 Optimal Income Tax

Having established this, we can now derive the optimal tax rules in a standard way, extending the procedure already employed several times so far. The expressions for the optimal marginal income tax rates are

$$T'\left(Y^{1L}\right) = \sum_h \left[\frac{\sigma^{h,1L} V_b^{h,1L}}{\mu}\left(\frac{V_y^{h,1L}}{V_b^{h,1L}} - \frac{V_y^{1L}}{V_b^{1L}}\right)\right] + \\ - \left\{t_z \tilde{Z}_y^{1L} + B^{1L} \tilde{N}_y^{1L}\right\}, \quad h = 1H, 2L, 2H; \tag{6.25}$$

$$T'\left(Y^{2L}\right) = \sum_h \left[\frac{\sigma^{h,2L} V_B^{h,2L}}{\mu}\left(\frac{V_Y^{h,2L}}{V_B^{h,2L}} - \frac{V_Y^{2L}}{V_B^{2L}}\right)\right] - \left\{t_z \tilde{Z}_y^{2L} + B^{1L} \tilde{N}_y^{2L}\right\}, \quad h = 1H, 2H; \tag{6.26}$$

$$T'\left(Y^{1H}\right) = \frac{\sigma^{2H,1H} V_B^{2H,1H}}{\mu}\left(\frac{V_Y^{2H,1H}}{V_B^{2H,1H}} - \frac{V_Y^{1H}}{V_B^{1H}}\right) - \left\{t_z \widehat{Z}_y^{1H} + B^{1L} \widehat{N}_y^{1H}\right\}; \tag{6.27}$$

$$T'\left(Y^{2H}\right) = -\left\{t_z \tilde{Z}_y^{2H} + B^{1L} \tilde{N}_y^{2H}\right\}, \tag{6.28}$$

where the "tilde" denotes a Hicksian demand.

The interpretation is also standard: just as we did for (6.18) and (6.19), suppose for a moment that no taxes on children or commodities are at hand, so that the term in curly brackets in each expression is identically zero. Then, we immediately see that $T'(y^{2H}) = 0$, which coincides with the familiar no-distortion-at-the-top property, while all the other tax rates will be non-zero. As always, in the presence of mimicking, a non-zero marginal rate of income tax will favour self-selection, by making the tax package intended for the mimicked less attractive for the mimicker. Since nobody is interested in mimicking $2H$-households, there is no point in distorting their labour/leisure trade-off; instead, for the other three household types it is useful to introduce this distortion.

Whether this should be achieved by taxing or subsidising income at the margin, depends on whether the mimicker dislikes working more or less than the mimicked does. For example, if $(\sigma^{2H,1H} V_b^{2H,1H})/\mu > 0$, we see that $T'(y^{1H}) > 0$ if, at the optimal (y^{1H}, b^{1H}), the indifference curve of the $(2H, 1H)$-mimicker are steeper than that of the genuine $1H$-household in the (y, b)-plane (the terms in parentheses are marginal rates of substitution between y and b, that is the gradients of the indifference curves). If the mimicker can be compensated with a smaller increase in after-tax income than the mimicked for any given increase in pre-tax income (which equals labour supply up to a constant—the wage rate), then it pays to impose a positive marginal rate of income tax on the latter, since this is what will make its tax treatment less attractive for the former. The same reasoning applies to the tax rates concerning $1L$- and $2L$-households, although in those cases there might be countervailing forces in action, as one mimicker might dislike working more, and another less, than the mimicked; the sign of the marginal income tax rates will therefore depend on the net effect.

Just as in the two-types scenario, there is also a revenue effect, reflected by the terms in curly brackets in (6.25)–(6.28) that provides an additional, and independent, reason for distortionary income taxation. This is particularly evident in the case of the $2H$-households, that are not mimicked by any of the other; if for example $\left[t_z \widehat{Z}_y^{2H} + B^{1L} \widehat{N}_y^{2H}\right] < 0$, then the revenue from taxing commodities and number of children falls as the labour supply of type-$2H$ households goes up. Then, although nobody is interested in mimicking these households, imposing a positive marginal rate of income tax on them would then raise tax revenue.

6.4.2 *Optimal Indirect Taxes and Taxes on Children*

We can now characterise the tax treatment of child-specific commodities and of quantity as follows:

$$\sum_h n^h \left(t_z \widehat{Z}_{t_z}^h + B^h \widehat{Z}_B^h\right) = N^{1L} \sum_{k=1H,2L,2H} \frac{\sigma^{k,1L} V_b^{k,1L}}{\mu} n^k (z^{1L} - z^{k,1L}) +$$
$$+ N^{2L} \sum_{k=1H,2H} \frac{\sigma^{k,2L} V_b^{k,2L}}{\mu} n^k (z^{2L} - z^{k,2L}) + N^{1H} \frac{\sigma^{2H,1H} V_b^{2H,1H}}{\mu} n^k (z^{1H} - z^{2H,1H}), \tag{6.29}$$

and

$$t_z \widehat{N}_{t_z}^h + B^h \widehat{N}_B^h = 0, \quad i = 1L, 1H, 2L, 2H, \tag{6.30}$$

where (6.30) is of course identical to (6.20) and has the same interpretation. As for (6.29), it is a variant of (6.21), and the interpretation is also familiar: the demand for child-specific commodities is "discouraged" ("encouraged") if, on the whole, the mimickers consume more of z than the mimicked. It is then clear that, in this case, distorting prices in favour of adult-specific commodities would harm the mimickers more than the mimicked. Therefore, the self-selection constraints can be relaxed by discouraging Z.

6.4.3 The Tax Treatment of Children and Child-Specific Goods

In order to discuss the implications of the rules (6.29) and (6.30) for the design of taxation, it may be useful to focus on a simplified case which brings out the most innovative aspects of our approach. If we assume that parental time λ enters separably in the quality function, and that the utility function is also separable in its three arguments x, Q and N, we then have that the allocation of disposable income between x and z does not depend on w. Indeed, by imposing the above structure on the quality and utility functions, we replicate the situation arising in standard consumer models without home-production when non-labour time ("leisure") is weakly separable from the other goods. We recreate, then, the situation of the Atkinson and Stiglitz (1976) theorem on direct vs. indirect taxation, which states (in a conventional setting, without household production and with agents differing only for their wage rates) that when non-working time is weakly separable from the other goods, non-income taxes are redundant at the optimum—the general income tax is enough to achieve the desired amount of redistribution.

In the present setup, however, even when the demands for x and Z are independent from w, they may still depend on a. Recall that mimickers have the same disposable income and the same fertility level as the mimicked (disposable income is the same because pre-tax income and tax liability are the same). But, as long as they have different a's, they will still have different spending patterns. Therefore, indirect taxation will have some screening power, i.e. t_z and, consequently, B^h will be non-zero at the optimum. Then, the Atkinson-Stiglitz theorem does not apply—it may be optimal to tax (subsidise) child-specific commodities and the number of children, as well as income, even if the allocation of disposable income does not depend on the time allocation. To see this, we simply check the sign of the r.h.s. of (6.29). Since w does not matter, households with the same a will consume the same amount of z, and the rule reduces to

$$\sum_h n^h \left(t_z \tilde{Z}^h_{t_z} + B^h \tilde{Z}^h_B \right) = N^{1L} \sum_{k=1H,2H} \frac{\sigma^{k,1L} V_b^{k,1L}}{\mu} n^k (z^{1L} - z^{k,1L}) + \\ + N^{2L} \sum_{k=1H,2H} \frac{\sigma^{k,2L} V_b^{k,2L}}{\mu} n^k (z^{2L} - z^{k,2L}), \tag{6.31}$$

that is the last term on the r.h.s. and one of the addends in the first summation on the r.h.s. vanish. The outcome then will depend only on whether the demand for z is increasing or decreasing in a. In the first case, Z will be discouraged, because the mimickers consume more of it than the mimicked. In the second case, Z will be encouraged, since now the mimicked will have more taste for it than the mimickers.

For each of these two cases, the sign of B^h will then depend on whether Z and N are Hicksian substitutes or complements. For example, suppose that the demand for z goes up as a increases; then, by (6.31),

$$\sum_{h}^{h} \left(t_z \widehat{Z}^h_{t_z} + B^h \widehat{Z}^h_B\right) = 0. \tag{6.32}$$

We know that $\widehat{Z}^h_{t_z} < 0$ by the negativity of the own-price Slutsky term; if we further suppose that Z is a substitute for N in the Hicksian sense, then $\widehat{Z}^h_B > 0$. Since Hicksian substitutability between Z and N implies that t_z and B^h have the same sign (see above), and the own-price effect $\widehat{Z}^h_{t_z}$ is likely to dominate the cross-price effect $\widehat{Z}^h_B$, then the only possibility is that they are both positive. Similar reasoning will help us to sign t_z and B^h for all the other possible cases. Again, we cannot conclude that children should necessarily be subsidised, i.e. we do not find unconditional support for the usual belief that large families should be directly compensated by the tax system.[8] It may be the case, but it is just as possible that the number of children will be taxed.

6.5 Conclusions

In the model studied in this Chapter, we considered two elements that have a major impact on the tax analysis. First, households are differentiated by their ability in the domestic production of a non-tradable good, children, as well as by their ability in the labour market. Second, fertility is endogenous, which leads us naturally to identify domestic ability with a lower fixed cost of raising children.

In the two-types scenario, the first element introduces the possibility that re-distribution will be from low to high-utility households. That may happen even in the presence of explicit inequality aversion, but is obviously more likely if the welfare function is Benthamite. The reason for this apparent paradox is that allocative efficiency requires households to specialize according to *comparative advantage*, and that, as children are not tradeable, specialization in domestic production (child rearing) is restricted by the need to raise income in order to pay for the (child-specific) commodities used as input. Therefore, re-distribution in favour of households with a comparative advantage in raising children may well raise welfare, even if the

[8] We cannot rule out, however, that they are subsidised in a indirect manner. Recall that the marginal cost of a child is affected by all the policy instruments.

beneficiaries happen to have an *absolute advantage* in domestic production large enough to give them higher *laissez-faire* utility than the rest of the population.[9]

Since children are observable at zero marginal cost, recognizing that fertility is the result of choice gives the policy maker a considerable advantage in the design of an optimal system of taxes and transfers. In a context where the government does not observe, or can only discover at high cost, the characteristics of adult household members, fertility behaviour does in fact convey a great deal of information about those characteristics, which helps to relax the self-selection constraints on the design of policy.

Together, the two aforementioned elements lead to some unconventional policy prescriptions. One is that it may *not* be optimal to design the tax system so that an additional child would lighten the net tax burden on his or her parents. Another unconventional result is that, if it is optimal to encourage parents to have more children, that should be done indirectly, by distorting prices in favour of child-specific commodities through differential taxation, or by reducing the opportunity-cost of parental time through a positive marginal income tax rate, rather than by a straight subsidy on the number of children (child benefits). Indeed, the number of children should be taxed (negative child benefits), to counter the distortion of the quantity-quality trade-off, if other policy instruments are used to raise the incentive to have children.

These conclusions carry over to the the four-type scenario. For that specific scenario (but the analysis would have lead to the same conclusions in the two-type setup), we also made a comparison with the well-know Atkinson and Stiglitz (1976) theorem. We noted, as we already did for a comparable framework in Chap. 2, that the theorem does not apply: as long as households differ along more dimensions that just the wage rate (domestic ability in our case), non-income taxes, including taxes on the number of children, should be used also when the required separability condition is met.

---

[9] As we saw in Chap. 2, that is a general property of models with households differing in market and non-market skills and home-production of non-tradeable goods.

Chapter 7
The Tax Treatment of Children When Parents Act Non-cooperatively: A Preliminary Account

7.1 Introduction

In this brief final chapter we will investigate, once again, the question of whether children should be a tax asset or a tax liability to their parents, in a context however where the parents act non-cooperatively. This is a novelty, to the best of our knowledge—the literature, as we saw, either focuses on the interaction of the members of a couple when decisions concerning home-production (typically of a household public good) must be taken, *or* on the fertility behaviour under the assumption that they act unitarily. This is of course a reasonable modelling strategy; still, it is interesting to see what happens when the two perspectives are merged. Here we provide a first, tentative answer, and ponder on the difficulties of finding an appropriate way of representing the situation in a way which is both manageable and not too far-fetched with respect to the main stylised facts relative to marriage and fertility. We start with a model in which fertility is endogenous and the consider briefly the possibility of extending the results to a model of endogenous fertility. We find that the case for subsidising children is not clear-cut, even with exogenous fertility, due to the non-cooperative behaviour of the parents.

7.2 A Model with Exogenous Fertility

Consider an economy with two types of agents, $h = 1, 2$ differentiated by their wage rate or market productivity w, such that $w^2 > w^1$; there are n^h agents of each type. The total number of agents is normalised to unity, and $n^1 = n^2 = 1/2$. Agent live in two-people households in which one of the partners is a high-wager and the other is a low-wager; they rely on a marketed composite good for private consumption, x^h, and have an exogenously determined number N^h of identical children whose quality (of life) Q is achieved by using two domestically produced commodities which we

A. Balestrino, *The Economics of Family Taxation*, Population Economics,
https://doi.org/10.1007/978-3-031-28170-9_7

call "parental attention" (one for each parent, obviously) and, in turn, are obtained via a marketed input z^h (specific children commodities) combined with the partner's own time λ^h:

$$\rho^h = \rho\left(z^h, \lambda^h\right). \tag{7.1}$$

We assume ρ to be strictly concave, increasing in both its arguments, and to exhibit constant returns to scale as well as weak technological complementarity, i.e. $\partial\rho/\partial z^k \partial\lambda^k \geq 0$.The total time endowment is normalised to unity and the time left-over from child-rearing is devoted to market work, l^h and l^k. Assuming for simplicity that the two partners' parental attentions are perfectly substitutable with each other and that they enter the quality function linearly, $Q = \rho^h + \rho^k$, utility is then

$$U^h = U(x^h, \rho^h + \rho^k; N^h),\ h, k = 1, 2; h \neq k \tag{7.2}$$

The utility function is also taken to be strictly concave. As in previous chapters, the production sector is made of constant-returns-to-scale firms that use labour as their only input. The budget constraint and the time constraint are, respectively:

$$x^h + q_z N^h z^h = (1 - \tau)w^h l^h + BN^h + T \text{ and } N^h \lambda^h + l^h = 1,\ h = 1, 2, \tag{7.3}$$

where units are chosen so that pre-tax prices all equal unity, $q_z = 1 + t_z$ is the after-tax price of z with t_z denoting the indirect tax rate, $\tau \in (0, 1)$ is the marginal rate of income tax, $B > 0$ is a per-child subsidy (a "demogrant") and $T > 0$ is the lump-sum subsidy; the tax on x has been normalised to zero (see Chap. 1). Thus, income is taxed linearly, with a constant marginal tax rate and a uniform subsidy that provides a progressivity effect. As we know, since only relative prices (and relative tax rates) matter, the good whose tax rate is set to zero serves as a benchmark: one should interpret a positive (negative) tax rate on another good as an indication that the latter is to be taxed more heavily (leniently) than the benchmark one. We start from a situation in which $t_z = B = 0$ and then explore the implications of raising either one of them under the obligation to keep revenue unchanged, i.,e. with a compensatory adjustment in the level of another policy instrument, which for simplicity is taken to be T.

In this formulation, $Q = \rho^h + \rho^k$ can be usefully thought of as a household public good: both partners enjoy their children's quality of life in a non-exclusive and non-rivalrous way. In line with the way we modelled the agents' behaviour in Chap. 3, we assume that each person decides how to allocate his or her time and his or her budget taking the other person's contributions to the household good as given: that is, agents have Cournot conjectures about the behavior of the other member of the household. Since however what ultimately matters to the agent is the "consumption" of the "household public good", it might be helpful to represent the maximisation problem in such a way to highlight the role of ρ, i.e. of the constituents of Q, rather than that of the inputs into the production of ρ. To this end, we divide the consumer's problem in two steps. In the first, she minimises the cost of producing ρ, that is, she chooses z^h and λ^h so as to

$$\min q_z z^h + (1-\tau)w^h\lambda^h \text{ s.t. } \rho(z^h,\lambda^h) \geq \overline{\rho},\ \left(\pi^h\right), h,k=1,2;\ h \neq k; \quad (7.4)$$

the Lagrange multiplier is in parentheses. The first order conditions are

$$q_z = \pi^h \frac{\partial \rho^h}{\partial z^h};\ (1-\tau)w^h = \pi^h \frac{\partial \rho^h}{\partial \lambda^h}. \quad (7.5)$$

Let the minimum value function (expenditure function) descending from these problems be

$$C^h = C\left(\rho^h; q_z, (1-\tau)w^h\right); \quad (7.6)$$

by the envelope theorem,

$$\pi^h\left(q_z, (1-\tau)w^h\right) = \frac{\partial C^h}{\partial \overline{\rho}}. \quad (7.7)$$

Then, π^h can be interpreted as the "price" of parental attention.[1] Due to our assumptions of constant returns to scale and technological complementarity, it depends positively on q_z and w^h (and, clearly, negatively on τ), but does *not* depend on the level of ρ^h, as can be deduced by a straightforward comparative statics exercise:

$$\frac{\partial \pi^h}{\partial q_z} > 0;\ \frac{\partial \pi^h}{\partial w^h} = -\frac{\partial \pi^h}{\partial \tau} > 0;\ \frac{\partial \pi^h}{\partial \overline{\rho}} = 0. \quad (7.8)$$

The first two signs are driven by the assumption of weak technological complementarity—only sufficient, not necessary. The third instead requires linear homogeneity of $Q(\cdot)$; its proof can be based on the fact that, as a consequence, the marginal productivities are homogeneous of degree zero. This is indeed an intuitively appealing, and at the same time manageable, scenario: the price of parental attention increases with the prices of its inputs, but, due to constant returns to scale, does not vary with the produced quantity, which, in turn, implies that in terms of the policy variables, the price of parental attention rises with the tax on the children's good and falls with the income tax rate (the lump-sum transfers have no effect).

In order to define the second step of the maximisation problem, let us first substitute the time constraint into the budget constraint so as to write

$$x^h + q_z N^h z^h + (1-\tau)w^h N^h \lambda^h = (1-\tau)w^h + BN^h + T, \quad (7.9)$$

and then use the expenditure function (7.6) to write

$$x^h + N^h C\left(Q^h; q_z, (1-\tau)w^h\right) = (1-\tau)w^h + BN^h + T. \quad (7.10)$$

---

[1] In our formulation π^h could also be thought of as the "price" of quality, since the latter is just the sum of parental attentions, were not for the fact that there would be two prices of quality, one for each parent.

Then substitute the budget constraint into the utility function:

$$U^h = U(((1-\tau)w^h + BN^h + T) - N^h C\left(\rho^h; q_z, (1-\tau)w^h\right), \rho^h + \rho^k; N^h). \tag{7.11}$$

The second stage than can be described as the choice of ρ^h so as to maximise the above utility function, under the assumption of Cournot conjectures, i.e. that each partner chooses his or her level of parental attention taking the level of the other partner's parental attention as given. This yields the FOC

$$-U_x^h N^h \pi^h + U_\rho^h = 0. \tag{7.12}$$

Solving (7.12) gives us the reaction functions $\rho^h = f(\lambda^k; q_z, \tau, T)$ and, symmetrically, $\rho^k = f(\lambda^h; q_z, \tau, T, B)$, where we highlighted the policy tools among the arguments. A Nash-Cournot equilibrium is a pair $\left(\widehat{\rho}^h, \widehat{\rho}^k\right)$ such that

$$\widehat{\rho}^h = f\left(\widehat{\rho}^k; q_z, \tau, T, B\right); \quad \widehat{\rho}^k = f\left(\widehat{\rho}^h; q_z, \tau, T, B\right), h, k = 1, 2; h \neq k. \tag{7.13}$$

We can now, once again, rely on two standard results from the literature on the private provision of public goods. As we know, Bergstrom et al. (1986, 1992) have shown that if preferences are strictly convex, which we assume to be the case, and both x and ρ are normal, as we also assume, then the Nash-Cournot equilibrium exists and is unique. Second, non-cooperative behavior generates underprovision: both agents would be better-off if the provision level were increased, but since each partner does not acknowledge the fact that his or her contribution to the public good benefits the other partner, underprovision will prevail at the market equilibrium.

The indirect utility function will be denoted as

$$V^h = V(q_z, \tau, T, B), \tag{7.14}$$

where we have again chosen to highlight the policy instruments among the arguments. Then, applying the envelope theorem twice and taking into account the Nash-Cournot interactions, we have

$$\frac{\partial V^h}{\partial q_z} = -U_x^h N^h z^h + U_Q^h \frac{\partial \rho^k}{\partial q_z} < 0; \tag{7.15}$$

$$\frac{\partial V^h}{\partial \tau} = U_x^h(-w^h + w^h N^h \lambda^h) + U_Q^h \frac{\partial \rho^k}{\partial \tau} = -U_x^h w^h l^h + U_Q^h \frac{\partial \rho^k}{\partial \tau}; \tag{7.16}$$

$$\frac{\partial V}{\partial T} = U_x^h + U_Q^h \frac{\partial \rho^k}{\partial T} > 0; \tag{7.17}$$

$$\frac{\partial V}{\partial B} = N^h U_x^h + U_Q^h \frac{\partial \rho^k}{\partial B} > 0 \tag{7.18}$$

where the signs are determined using the following:

$$\frac{\partial \rho^k}{\partial q_z} = \frac{\partial \rho^k}{\partial z^k}\frac{\partial z^k}{\partial q_z} + \frac{\partial \rho^k}{\partial \lambda^k}\frac{\partial \lambda^k}{\partial q_z} < 0; \quad (7.19)$$

$$\frac{\partial \rho^k}{\partial \tau} = \frac{\partial \rho^k}{\partial z^k}\frac{\partial z^k}{\partial \tau} + \frac{\partial \rho^k}{\partial \lambda^k}\frac{\partial \lambda^k}{\partial \tau} > 0; \quad (7.20)$$

$$\frac{\partial \rho^k}{\partial T} = \frac{\partial \rho^k}{\partial z^k}\frac{\partial z^k}{\partial T} + \frac{\partial \rho^k}{\partial \lambda^k}\frac{\partial \lambda^k}{\partial T} > 0; \quad (7.21)$$

$$\frac{\partial \rho^k}{\partial B} = \frac{\partial \rho^k}{\partial z^k}\frac{\partial z^k}{\partial B} + \frac{\partial \rho^k}{\partial \lambda^k}\frac{\partial \lambda^k}{\partial B} > 0, \quad (7.22)$$

which, in turn, descend from the assumptions that all goods are normal in income (including home-time) and z and λ are gross complements (as well as technological complements). As expected, then, utility is impacted negatively by a rise in the consumer price of (the tax rate on) z or the marginal rate of income tax, and positively by a rise in the poll-tax or in the demogrant; the impact of the tax rate is instead ambiguous because, on the one hand, it has a direct negative effect on utility, on the other hand, however, it increases the partner's contribution to quality (the household public good) by discouraging his or her labour supply. The ambiguity of this result is interesting because it highlights how also the effect from the other policy tools is twofold: they impact on the agent's utility both in immediate terms and *via* the variation in the partner's contribution to quality. In all cases, except that of the income tax rate, the two components of the total effect agree in sign, but they should be kept separate from a logical viewpoint.

For future reference, we also state here the results of the comparative statics at the Nash-Cournot equilibrium:

$$\frac{\partial \rho^h}{\partial q_z} = -\frac{-U^h_{xx}(-N^h z^h)N^h\pi^h - U^h_x N^h(\partial \pi^h/\partial q_z)}{U^h_{\rho\rho}} < 0; \quad (7.23)$$

$$\frac{\partial \rho^h}{\partial \tau} = -\frac{-U^h_{xx}(-w^h l^h)N^h\pi^h - U^h_x N^h(\partial \pi^h/\partial \tau)}{U^h_{\rho\rho}}; \quad (7.24)$$

$$\frac{\partial \rho^h}{\partial T} = -\frac{-U^h_{xx}N^h\pi^h}{U^h_{\rho\rho}} > 0; \quad (7.25)$$

$$\frac{\partial \rho^h}{\partial B} = -\frac{-U^h_{xx}\left(N^h\right)^2\pi^h}{U^h_{\rho\rho}} > 0. \quad (7.26)$$

7.2.1 Revenue-Neutral Fiscal Reforms

We now investigate the effects of introducing revenue-neutral reforms, whereby one of the fiscal instruments is marginally increased while another is adjusted so as to leave total revenue unchanged. We study the introduction of a tax on children commodities as well as of a demogrant (it will be recalled that both were zero to begin with, whereas the income tax was in place); T is modified to compensate the ensuing variation in the government's budget.

Let us begin by stating the public budget constraint:

$$R \equiv t_z(n^1N^1z^1 + n^2N^2z^2) + \tau(n^1w^1l^1 + n^2w^2l^2) - T - (n^1N^1 + n^2N^2)B = 0. \tag{7.27}$$

If we modify $t_z$and T as we described above, we must have

$$\left.\frac{\partial R}{\partial t_z}\right|_{t_z=0} dt_z - \left.\frac{\partial R}{\partial T}\right|_{t_z=0} dT = 0; \tag{7.28}$$

We have

$$\frac{\partial R}{\partial t_z} = \overleftrightarrow{Z} + t_z\frac{\partial \overleftrightarrow{Z}}{\partial t_z} + \tau\frac{\partial \overleftrightarrow{L}}{\partial t_z} > 0, \tag{7.29}$$

where $\overleftrightarrow{Z}$ is the aggregate consumption of z, i.e. $n^1N^1z^1 + n^2N^2z^2$ and $\overleftrightarrow{L}$ is defined similarly; the sign follows from the fact that home-time and child consumption are gross complements (and the assumption that $\tau > 0$; also recall that we are evaluating the derivative at $t_z = B = 0$). Also, we have

$$\frac{\partial R}{\partial T} = t_z\frac{\partial \overleftrightarrow{Z}}{\partial T} + \tau\frac{\partial \overleftrightarrow{L}}{\partial T} < 0, \tag{7.30}$$

where the signs follows from normality of home-time in income (and the fact that we are evaluating the derivative at $t_z = 0$). We conclude than that

$$\frac{dT}{dt_z} = -\frac{\partial R/\partial t_z}{\partial R/\partial T} > 0, \tag{7.31}$$

meaning that the introduction of a tax rate on child commodities requires an increase in the lump-sum subsidy to balance the budget: the extra-revenue from the indirect tax is compensated by a reduction in the tax base for the direct tax (reduced labour supply). Overall, then, the tax on z seems to enhance the redistributive impact of the income tax. To give a more comprehensive answer to the question of what is the overall impacts of introducing a tax on z, however, we need to look at the effects on social welfare.

To this end, let us define a standard quasi-concave social welfare function:

$$W = W(n^1V^1 + n^2V^2). \tag{7.32}$$

Note then that

$$\frac{\partial W}{\partial t_z} = n^1\left(W_1\frac{\partial V^1}{\partial t_z} + W_1\frac{\partial V^1}{\partial T}\frac{\partial T}{\partial t_z}\right) + n^2\left(W_2\frac{\partial V^2}{\partial t_z} + W_2\frac{\partial V^2}{\partial T}\frac{\partial T}{\partial t_z}\right), \tag{7.33}$$

where $W_h = \partial W / \partial V^h > 0$, $h = 1, 2$ (the "welfare weights"). Using (7.15), (7.17) and (7.31) it is easy to see that, in each parenthesis, the first term is negative, while the second is positive. The overall effect is then ambiguous.

Visually, it might help to re-write (7.33) as follows:

$$\frac{\partial W}{\partial t_z} = \left(n^1 W_1 \frac{\partial V^1}{\partial t_z} + n^2 W_2 \frac{\partial V^2}{\partial t_z} \right) + \left(n^1 W_1 \frac{\partial V^1}{\partial T} \frac{\partial T}{\partial t_z} + n^2 W_2 \frac{\partial V^2}{\partial T} \frac{\partial T}{\partial t_z} \right), \quad (7.34)$$

so that now the first term is negative and the second is positive. The first term registers the immediate impact of an increase in the tax rate, which is clearly negative; the second term, however, registers a positive indirect impact, as the increase in the poll subsidy due the necessity to balance the budget brings about, as we saw, a fall in the labour supply and, consequently, a rise in the supply of parental attention, which we know is inefficiently low to begin with (due to the Nash-Cournot behaviour). So, providing care is going to cost a little more, due to the tax on z, but the overall supply of parental attention might increase and the provision of the household public good Q may rise as a result. If that is the case, a tax on z is actually welfare-improving.

Of course, this need not be the case: the direct impact may prevail. But, once again, we find that subsidising the cost of raising children is far from being a foregone conclusion. This is is all the more remarkable here because fertility is exogenous, and we usually found that the case for child subsidies is much stronger in that case: here, however, it is the inefficiency built in in the family behaviour that drives the result.

Let us now consider the introduction of a demogrant. If we modify B and T so as to leave total revenue unaffected, we must have

$$\left.\frac{\partial R}{\partial B}\right|_{B=0} dB - \left.\frac{\partial R}{\partial T}\right|_{B=0} dT = 0. \quad (7.35)$$

Then

$$\frac{\partial R}{\partial B} = -\overleftrightarrow{N} + t_z \frac{\partial \overleftrightarrow{Z}}{\partial B} + \tau \frac{\partial \overleftrightarrow{L}}{\partial B} < 0, \quad (7.36)$$

where $\overleftrightarrow{N}$ is the aggregate number of children. Since, once again, we are evaluating the derivative under the assumption that $\tau > 0$ and at $t_z = B = 0$, the sign follows from normality of home-time in income (the demogrant, under endogenous fertility, is simply lump sum income). We conclude than that

$$\frac{dT}{dB} = -\frac{\partial R / \partial B}{\partial R / \partial T} = -\overleftrightarrow{N} < 0, \quad (7.37)$$

meaning that the introduction of a demogrant requires a decrease in the lump-sum subsidy to balance the budget: indeed, these are just two sources of lump-sum income for the family and revenue-neutrality obviously requires that if the demogrant is raised by one euro, the subsidy must be reduced by $\overleftrightarrow{N}$ euros. Finally, we write

$$\frac{\partial W}{\partial B} = n^1 \left(W_1 \frac{\partial V^1}{\partial B} + W_1 \frac{\partial V^1}{\partial T} \frac{\partial T}{\partial B} \right) + n^2 \left(W_2 \frac{\partial V^2}{\partial B} + W_2 \frac{\partial V^2}{\partial T} \frac{\partial T}{\partial B} \right), \quad (7.38)$$

or

$$\frac{\partial W}{\partial B} = n^1 W_1 \left(\frac{\partial V^1}{\partial B} - \frac{\partial V^1}{\partial T} \overleftrightarrow{N} \right) + n^2 W_2 \left(\frac{\partial V^2}{\partial B} - \frac{\partial V^2}{\partial T} \overleftrightarrow{N} \right) = 0, \quad (7.39)$$

where we used (7.17) and (7.18). This was of course to be expected: the lump-sum transfer T absorbs all other lump-sum transfers. If one were so inclined, one could however see this as another way of saying that, even under exogenous fertility, direct subsidisation of the number of children is useless: a comprehensive uniform subsidy achieves the same result. The behaviour of the parents plays no part in this result: it is all due to the internal logic of taxation applied to the case of exogenous fertility.

On the whole then, under the assumptions of exogenous fertility and non-cooperative behaviour of the parents, there is no strong case for a policy of subsidisation of the cost of raising children: taxes on child-related commodities might in principle be welfare-improving as they counteract the inefficiently low supply of parental attention (due to the Nash-Cournot behaviour) and subsidies linked to the number of children are superfluous.

7.3 Concluding Remarks: Moving Towards Endogenous Fertility

The introduction of endogenous fertility in the present context is not really straightforward, and the modelling strategy requires careful thought. This is mainly because the decision to have children is one-shot, whereas the decision to care for them is actually made of a sequence of decision to buy commodities and devote time over an extended period of time. So, assuming non-cooperative behaviour makes sense for the latter, as childcare requires a sustained commitment and the impossibility of writing binding contracts makes a significant impact. Instead, once the decision of having children is taken and acted upon, it usually ends with the desired result in a few months's time (nine, actually). Decision reversal is costly, as abortions, even when they are legally available, are really not an easy choice, emotionally and sometimes financially. Of course, there may be involuntary pregnancies as well as failures to have one: in the vast majority of cases, however, the kind of commitment required to have a child is at a different level from the one required for raising one. So, if we use, as we do, a static model in which a lifetime of choices is constricted in a single moment, we need some way to differentiate the two types of decisions.

One possibility is to imagine that while the decision to have children is taken cooperatively, that is to say, unitarily, by the couple, the decisions involved in providing them with the care they need are taken non-cooperatively. The overall maximisation problem of the household would then involve two stages: in the first, the level of fertility, i.e. the number of children, is chosen; in the second, the children's quality of life is chosen (this latter stage can be described in two steps as we did earlier). If we solve this problem backward, we could then assume that the couple goes through the second stage, which would be identical to the process described in the previous section, for all the different possible levels of fertility. These could be finite and discrete: $0, 1, 2 \ldots N^{\max}$ where $N^{\max}$ would be, of course, the maximum fertility level (which could also be household-specific). Then, the couple would choose the fertility level which maximises their utility. If N were a continuous number, the optimal level, say N^*, would be identified by solving

$$U_N + U_x\ B = U_x C(\cdot). \tag{7.40}$$

In the proposed setting, the optimal N would be the one closest to N^*.

The analysis of the fiscal reforms would then be similar to the one above. As long as the reform is marginal and does not induce a shift from one level of fertility to another, also the same results apply. If, however, we were to consider global, as opposed to local, results, i.e. optimal polices instead of reforms, then we would have to consider the impact of the policy instruments on the fertility choices. Clearly if either B or $C(\cdot)$ increase substantially in (7.40), then the optimal level of fertility would be affected.

In this final chapter, however, we will not explore this case in any detail. Our intent was simply to offer a preliminary explorations of the issues involved in building a model with endogenous fertility and non-cooperative parents for the study of the tax treatment of children. We leave the full elaboration of the model to future research efforts.

Bibliography

Altonji, J., Hayashi, F., & Kotlikoff, L. (1992). Is the extended family altruistically linked? Direct tests using micro data. *American Economic Review, 82,* 1177–98.
Altonji, J., Hayashi, F., & Kotlikoff, L. (1997). Parental altruism and inter vivos transfers: Theory and evidence. *Journal of Political Economy, 105,* 1121–66.
Anderberg, D., Andersson, F., & Balestrino, A. (2000). Time, self-selection and user charges for public goods. *FinanzArchiv, 57,* 137–154.
Anderberg, D., & Balestrino, A. (2000). Household production and the design of the tax structure. *International Tax and Public Finance, 7,* 563–584.
Anderberg, D., & Balestrino, A. (2003). Self-enforcing intergenerational transfers and the provision of education. *Economica, 70,* 55–71.
Anderberg, D., & Balestrino, A. (2007). Non-cooperative households and the size and composition of public expenditure. *Economics of Governance, 8,* 61–81.
Anderberg, D., & Balestrino, A. (2011). Public spending and taxation with non- cooperative families. *CESifo Economic Studies, 57,* 259–282.
Apps, P., & Rees, R. (1988). Taxation and the household. *Journal of Public Economics, 35,* 355–369.
Apps, P., & Rees, R. (1999). On the taxation of trade within and between households. *Journal of Public Economics, 73,* 241–263.
Apps, P., & Rees, R. (2011). Optimal taxation and tax reform for two-earner house- holds. *CESifo Economic Studies, 57,* 283–304.
Apps, P., & Rees, R. (2018). Optimal family taxation and income inequality. *International Tax and Public Finance, 25,* 1093–1128.
Apps, P., & Rees, R. (2023). Household decision making. In K. F. Zimmermann (Ed.), *Handbook of labor, human resources, and population economics*. Springer.
Atkinson, A., & Stiglitz, J. (1976). The design of tax structure: Direct versus indirect taxation. *Journal of Public Economics, 1,* 97–119.
Atkinson, A., & Stiglitz, J. (1981). *Lectures on public economics*. McGraw-Hill.
Atkinson, A., & Stiglitz, J. (2015). *Lectures on public economics* (updated). Princeton University Press.
Atkinson, A. (1977). Optimal taxation and the direct versus indirect tax controversy. *Canadian Journal of Economics, 10,* 590–606.

A. Balestrino, *The Economics of Family Taxation*, Population Economics,
https://doi.org/10.1007/978-3-031-28170-9

Balestrino, A., Cigno, A., & Pettini, A. (2001). Self-selection, redistribution, and endogenous fertility. In M. Bordignon & D. Da Empoli (Eds.), *Politica fiscale, flessibilità dei mercati e crescita* (pp. 212–225). Franco Angeli.

Balestrino, A. (2001). On the optimal fiscal treatment of family size. *FinanzArchiv, 58,* 140–157.

Balestrino, A. (2004). Revisiting the equity-efficiency trade-off: Taxation with non-cooperative families. *FinanzArchiv, 60,* 515–531.

Balestrino, A. (2015). Family taxation, fertility, and horizontal equity: A political economy perspective. *Public Finance Review, 43,* 402–427.

Balestrino, A., Cigno, A., & Pettini, A. (2002). Endogenous fertility and the design of family taxation. *International Tax and Public Finance, 9,* 175–193.

Balestrino, A., Cigno, A., & Pettini, A. (2003). Doing wonders with an egg: Optimal re-distribution when households differ in market and non-market abilities. *Journal of Public Economic Theory, 5,* 1–20.

Barcena-Martín, E., Blazquez, M., & Moro-Egido, A. I. (2020). The role of income pooling and decision-making responsibilities in material deprivation. *Economic Modeling, 87,* 416–428.

Becker, G. (1981, 1993). *A treatise on the family*. Harvard University Press.

Becker, G. (1965). A theory of the allocation of time. *Economic Journal, 75,* 493–508.

Becker, G. (1974). A theory of social interactions. *Journal of Political Economy, 82,* 1063–1093.

Benabou, R. (2000). Unequal societies: Income distribution and the social contract. *American Economic Review, 90,* 96–129.

Bergstrom, T., Blume, L., & Varian, H. (1986). On the private provision of public goods. *Journal of Public Economics, 29,* 25–49.

Bergstrom, T., Blume, L., & Varian, H. (1992). Uniqueness of Nash equilibrium in the private provision of public goods. *Journal of Public Economics, 49,* 391–392.

Binmore, K., Rubinstein, A., & Wolinsky, A. (1986). The Nash bargaining solution in economic modelling. *Rand Journal of Economics, 17,* 176–188.

Blumkin, T., Margalioth, Y., & Sadka, E. (2015). The re-distributive role of child benefits revisited. *International Tax and Public Finance, 22,* 476–501.

Boadway, R., & Bruce, N. (1975). *Welfare economics*. Blackwell.

Boskin, M. J., & Sheshinski, E. (1983). Optimal tax treatment of the family. *Journal of Public Economics, 20,* 281–297.

Bourguignon, F., Browning, M., & Chiappori, P.-A. (2006). Efficient intra-household allocations and distribution factors: Implications and identification, CAM Working Papers no. 2006-02, University of Copenhagen.

Browning, M., & Chiappori, P.-A. (1998). Efficient intra-household allocations: A general characterization and empirical tests. *Econometrica, 66,* 1241–1278.

Browning, M., & Gørtz, M. (2012). Spending time and money within the household. *Scandinavian Journal of Economics, 114,* 1688–1704.

Chen, Z., & Woolley, F. (2001). A Cournot-Nash model of family decision making. *Economic Journal, 111,* 722–748.

Chiappori, P. -A. (1988). Rational household labour supply. *Econometrica, 56*, 63–89.

Chiappori, P. -A. (1992). Collective labour supply and welfare. *Journal of Political Economy, 100,* 437–467.

Chiappori, P.-A., Fortin, B., & Lacroix, G. (2002). Household labor supply, sharing rule and the marriage market. *Journal of Political Economy, 110,* 37–72.

Christiansen, V. (1984). Which commodity taxes should supplement the income tax? *Journal of Public Economics, 24,* 195–220.

Cigno, A. (1991). *Economics of the family*. Clarendon Press.

Cigno, A. (1986). Fertility and the tax-benefit system: A reconsideration of the theory of family taxation. *The Economic Journal, 96,* 1035–1051.

Cigno, A. (1993). Intergenerational transfers without altruism: Family, market and state. *European Journal of Political Economy, 9,* 505–18.

Cigno, A. (2001). Comparative advantage, observability, and the optimal tax treatment of families with children. *International Tax and Public Finance, 8,* 455–470.

Cigno, A. (2006). A constitutional theory of the family. *Journal of Population Economics, 19,* 259–283.

Cigno, A., Giannelli, G., & Rosati, F. (1998). Voluntary transfers among Italian house-holds: Altruistic and non-altruistic explanations. *Structural Changes and Economic Dynamics, 4,* 435–53.

Cigno, A., Giannelli, G., Rosati, F., & Vuri, D. (2006). Is there such a thing as a family constitution? A test based on credit rationing. *Review of the Economics of the Household, 4,* 183–204.

Cremer, H., Dellis, A., & Pestieau, P. (2003). Family size and optimal income taxation. *Journal of Population Economics, 16,* 37–54.

Cremer, H., Lozachmeur, J.-M., Mortando, D., & Roeder, K. (2016). Household bargaining and the design of couples taxation. *European Economic Review, 89,* 454–470.

Cremer, H., Lozachmeur, J.-M., & Pestieau, P. (2011). Income taxation of couples and the tax unit choice. *Journal of Population Economics, 25,* 763–788.

Cremer, H., Pestieau, P., & Rochet, J.-C. (2000). Direct versus indirect taxation: The design of the tax structure revisited. *International Economic Review, 42,* 781–799.

Dasgupta, P. (2000). Reproductive externalities and fertility behavior. *European Economic Review, 44,* 619–644.

Deaton, A., & Muellbauer, J. (1980). *Economics and consumer behaviour.* Cambridge University Press.

Edwards, J., Keen, M. & Tuomala, M. (1994). Income tax, commodity taxes and public good provision: A brief guide. *FinanzArchiv, 51,* 472–487.

Fernandez, R., & Rogerson, R. (1999). Education finance reform and investment in human capital: Lessons from California. *Journal of Public Economics, 74,* 327–350.

Glomm, G., & Ravikumar, B. (2003). Public education and income inequality European. *Journal of Political Economy, 19,* 289–300.

Greene, K. V., & Nikolaev, O. (1999). Voter participation and the redistributive state. *Public Choice, 98,* 213–26.

Gronau, R. (1977). Leisure, home-production, and work: The theory of the allocation of time revisited. *Journal of Political Economy, 85,* 1099–1123.

Gruber, J. (1994). Is making divorce easier bad for children? The long-run implications of unilateral divorce, NBER Working Paper no. 7968.

Ihori, T. (1996). International public goods and contribution productivity differentials. *Journal of Public Economics, 61,* 139–154.

Jargowsky, P. (1996). Take the money and run: Economic segregation in U.S. metropolitan areas. *American Sociological Review, 61,* 984–998.

Juster, F., & Staff, F. (1991). The allocation of time: Empirical finance behavioral models, and problems of measurement. *Journal of Economic Literature, 29,* 471–522.

Kleven, H., Richter, W. F., & Sørensen, P. B. (1999). Optimal taxation with household production. *Oxford Economic Papers, 52,* 584–594.

Konrad, K., & Lommerud, K.-E. (1995). Family policy with non-cooperative families. *Scandinavian Journal of Economics, 97,* 581–601.

Konrad, K., & Lommerud, K.-E. (2000). The bargaining family revisited. *Canadian Journal of Economics, 33,* 471–487.

Lou, S., & Klohnen, E. (2005). Assortative mating and marital quality in newlyweds: A couple-centered approach. *Journal of Personality and Social Psychology, 88,* 304–326.

Lundberg, S., & Pollak, R. (1993). Separate spheres bargaining and the marriage market. *Journal of Political Economy, 101,* 988–1010.

Lundberg, S., & Pollak, R. (1996). Bargaining and distribution in marriage. *Journal of Economic Perspectives, 10,* 139–158.

Lundberg, S., & Pollak, R. (2003). Efficiency in marriage. *Review of Economics of the Household, 1,* 153–167.

Lundberg, S., & Pollak, R. (2007). The American family and family economics. *Journal of Economic Perspectives, 21,* 3–26.

Lundberg, S., Pollak, R., & Wales, T. (1997). Do husband and wives pool their resources? Evidence from the U.K. child benefit. *Journal of Human Resources, 32,* 463–480.

Manser, M., & Brown, M. (1980). Marriage and household decision-making: A bargaining analysis. *International Economic Review, 21,* 31–44.

Mare, R. (1991). Five decades of educational assortative mating. *American Sociological Review, 56,* 15–32.

McElroy, M., & Horney, M. (1981). Nash bargained household decision-making. *International Economic Review, 22,* 333–349.

McGarry, K. (2000). Testing parental altruism: Implications of a dynamic model. NBER Working Paper no. 7593

Mirrlees, J. (1971). An exploration into the theory of optimum income taxation. *Review of Economic Studies, 38,* 175–208.

Mirrlees, J. (1976). Optimal tax theory: A synthesis. *Journal of Public Economics, 6,* 327–358.

Myles, G. (2012). *Public Economics*. Cambridge University Press.

Nava, M., Schroyen, F., & Marchand, M. (1996). Optimal fiscal and public expenditure policy in a two-class economy. *Journal of Public Economics, 61,* 119–137.

Nerlove, M., Razin, A., & Sadka, E. (1987). *Household and Economy: Welfare Economics of Endogenous Fertility*. Academic Press.

Pollak, R. (2003). Gary Becker's contributions to family and household economics. *Review of Economics of the Household, 1,* 111–141.

Ponthieux, S. (2013). *Income pooling and equal sharing within the household—What can we learn from the 2010 EU-SILC module?*. Eurostat.

Ramsey, F. P. (1927). A contribution to the theory of taxation. *Economic Journal, 37,* 47–61.

Rees, R. (2023). Family taxation. Cambridge Elements.

Robinson, M., et al. (2017). Genetic evidence of assortative mating in humans. *Nature Human Behaviour, 1,* 0016. https://doi.org/10.1038/s41562-016-0016.

Rosen, S. (1995). Public employment, taxes and the welfare state in Sweden, NBER Working Paper No. 5003.

Sandmo, A. (1990). Tax distortions and household production. *Oxford Economic Papers, 42,* 78–90.

Seade, J. (1982). On the sign of the optimum marginal income tax. *Review of Economic Studies, 49,* 637–643.

Stern, N. (1982). Optimum taxation with errors in administration. *Journal of Public Economics, 17,* 181–211.

Stiglitz, J. (1982). Self-selection and Pareto-efficient taxation. *Journal of Public Economics, 17,* 213–240.

Vermeulen, F. (2002). Collective household models: Principles and main results. *Journal of Economic Surveys, 16,* 533–564.

Wolley, F. (1988). A non-cooperative model of family decision-making, Discussion Paper TIDI no. 25, London School of Economics.

The manufacturer's authorised representative in the EU is Springer Nature Customer Service Centre GmbH, Europaplatz 3, 69115 Heidelberg, Germany. If you have any concerns regarding our products, please contact ProductSafety@springernature.com

Printed and bound by CPI Group (UK) Ltd, Croydon, CR0 4YY
01/10/2026
02225876-0002